"If our youth would harness just 10% of what you have written, they would be light years ahead in their life and career. Hope you sell a million copies!"

—Gregg Jackson, Chief Strategy Officer at Acceleron Learning

"I loved the concise presentation of material without having to read pages and pages of buildup and having to search for the nuggets. This book is filled with useful nuggets from some of the most successful people. Herein lies the key to successfully navigating the employment arena."

—Linda Morrissey, American Airlines Operations, Retired

"Very impressive—I found myself thinking of the different topics and if I had done them in my career. Some I had done consciously. Most I had done unconsciously. Some I missed doing and it cost me dearly. For a young person, this book is a helpful guide to understand the right path."

—Chuck Larson, Larson Leather Company

"It's a mini-masterpiece!! I wish it was required reading for EVERY young person!! It would make their lives so much easier!! I wish I had had this to read when I was young! Great book!"

—Sally Fallis, Pathology Department, Retired

"I am buying one of these books for all three of my children and making it required reading! What do you know now that you wished you had known when you started your career? This book accomplishes that for young people graduating from High School or College. It is packed with concise wisdom. Every paragraph would be a complete chapter in a 500 page book. It is a quick read for young people with short attention spans. It will jump start their career and benefit them over their entire life!"

—Kendall Helfenbein, Dallas CFO

CLASSROOM TO CAREER

STEPS TO SUCCESS IN THE WORKPLACE

ALAN L. OPPENHEIMER

Classroom to Career (Steps to Success in the Workplace)

Copyright © 2022 by Alan L. Oppenheimer, Dock Holiday Press

All rights reserved. No part of this publication may be reproduced, distributed, or transmitted in any form or by any means, including photocopying, recording, or other electronic or mechanical methods, without the prior written permission of the publisher, except in the case of brief quotations embodied in critical reviews and certain other noncommercial uses permitted by copyright law.

Because of the dynamic nature of the internet, any web address or links contained in this book may have changed since publication and may no longer by valid.

Editing by The Pro Book Editor
Interior and Cover Design by IAPS.rocks

eBook ISBN: 978-1-7350860-2-6
Paperback ISBN: 978-1-7350860-3-3

    Main category—EDUCATION/Professional Development
    Other category—BUSINESS & ECONOMICS/Workplace Culture
    Other category—SELF-HELP/Personal Growth/Success

Second Edition

Dedicated to Donna Kun, Richard Falk, and Jeanie Pemberton

TABLE OF CONTENTS

Introduction ... 1
PART I – Life after High School ... 5
    Should You Go to College? ... 7
    Mapping Your Career Path ... 16
    Matching Personality Traits and Talents to Career ... 25
    Matching Strengths and Interests to Career ... 29
    Hourly vs. Salary Mentality ... 32
    Salary, Wages, Compensation, and Your Major and Your College ... 36
    Summer Jobs ... 38
PART II – Getting and Keeping a Job ... 53
    Integrity ... 55
    Do the Right Thing ... 61
    Digital Manners ... 66

Sex, Religion, and Politics ... 71
Do You Need a Mentor? ... 75
Constructive Criticism ... 83
Question ... 86
MPG – Manage Your Professional Growth ... 90

PART III – Moving Up ... 93

Make Learning a Lifelong Journey ... 95
"How to Win Friends and
Influence People" ... 101
Attitude, Personality, and
Capacity to Learn ... 106
Trade Up to Bigger Problems ... 110
Two Heads Are Better Than One ... 113
When Something Goes Wrong ... 114
Don't Be an Enabler ... 118
Impostor Syndrome ... 120
Taking a Leadership Role ... 123
Coworkers No More ... 131
Navigating Corporate America I ... 134
Navigating Corporate America II ... 141

PART IV – Changing Jobs ... 149

Leaving a Job ... 151
When Career Plans Are Derailed ... 158
Navigating Corporate America III ... 163

PART V – Important General Concepts 167
    Dos and Don'ts 169
    Things That Matter 178
    Three Things to Know as You Grow 179
    Online Meeting and
    Collaborating Etiquette 181
    Dining Etiquette 185
    We Are a Work in Progress 190

Recommended Books 197

About the Author 198

Acknowledgments 199

INTRODUCTION

THE MOVIE *INTO THE WILD* is based on the true story of Christopher McCandless, who hitchhiked to Alaska to live in the wilderness after graduating from Emory University. Before this adventure, Christopher knew nothing about living in the wild, let alone Alaska. He refused to take advice from those with more experience, thinking he could figure it out on his own. Christopher died of starvation at age twenty-four while camping along a remote trail.

While *Classroom to Career* does not deal with life or death, it does deal with your career's success or failure. It provides tools, advice, and lessons learned over a lifetime in corporate America.

Open up and listen to those who have been there. They will help you avoid the pitfalls that can wreck a career. Take advantage of help from those offering a leg up in your journey.

YOU NEED TO READ THIS BOOK BECAUSE...

A grandfather asks his three grandkids, "If you had a crystal ball that could predict the future and guide you throughout your life, would you listen to it or put it in your closet?" All three children said that they would listen to the crystal ball.

Very pleased with the answer, the grandfather said, "That's good, because you do have a crystal ball. Your crystal ball is your mother, father, and grandparents. Listen to them and listen to others who have life experience and want to help you. They have seen things that you have not and understand how today's actions have long-term rewards and/or consequences."

After twelve, sixteen, or even more years focused on your education and expending precious resources—time, sweat, and money—you're ready to start your career. Welcome to a new world that will not always make sense. More often than not, the transition from working on an education to working toward building a career can be surprising and unsettling. You may not have learned anything in school about this new environment of policy, procedures, office politics, corporate speak, goals and objectives, and company vision.

This book provides insight and direction for dealing with many issues and conundrums you will encounter in the workplace. Why stumble through the discovery process of how things work when you can get a head start on the learning curve that exists anytime we start something new?

Most people with forty years of work experience behind them did not understand the environment they were entering after their formal education ended. The advice presented in this book is meant to inspire discussions about your career path, help you with planning, and teach you how to measure your success. This book is the "easy button" so you can benefit from the experiences of a variety of successful managers and executives without having to make the same mistakes.

A retired buddy of mine said that while reading this book, he found himself thinking of the different topics and whether or not he had successfully addressed them in his career. Some he had addressed correctly, while others were a big miss that cost him dearly. For someone just starting out, this book is a helpful guide to understand the right path. For a more experienced person, it can be clarification in your own mind and an analysis of hits and misses in the workplace.

As you read this book, you may wonder if it is okay to skip chapters if the subject matter does not apply to your situation. For example, if you are about to graduate from college, why read the chapter on "Should You Go to College?" Sure, feel free to skip, but you may miss insights that might be helpful to pass on to a sibling or a friend.

You may think that your challenges are greater than those of generations before you. Am I right? It's natural—every generation feels this way until they gain enough life/work experience to broaden their viewpoint.

In a world of constant, rapid change, I thought my parents were dinosaurs. As I was coming of age, it seemed they didn't know what was going on in the world. I entered the workforce in 1976 with much the same perspective that you may have now. With time and experience, I learned that while parents and others a generation or more ahead of me may not be current on the latest technology, they have a wealth of experience in the world of work, which is largely behavioral- and relationship-based. Human relations change very slowly.

Life exposes us to many experiences, some of which I've gathered from my involvement in the corporate environment. My intention is to pay it forward and make a positive impact in your life. One note regarding perspective: numerous business professionals reviewed this book as well as provided material. These professionals felt the information provided was spot on and reflective of what they experienced in their professional careers. As you read the chapters, you may be surprised at some of the topics as well as the conclusions. Whether you agree, disagree, or are surprised by the material, file the material in your memory bank; you may need it one day.

PART I
LIFE AFTER HIGH SCHOOL

SHOULD YOU GO TO COLLEGE?

THIS CHAPTER IS INTENDED TO broaden your perspective on options other than college as well as the costs/benefits of college so that you can choose wisely.

College or graduate school is a wonderful thing for many people, as it prepares you for careers that require a college education or a graduate degree. But is college right for you? Some students attend college but never graduate, or they take courses that have little marketability. Worst of all, they accumulate significant debt that hangs over their heads for years.

A good place to start would be talking with your high school guidance counselor. Talk about what you want to do and what you do not want to do. If this discussion points to college, your next step should be to carefully look at the cost and anticipated debt at graduation. For the 2018–2019 academic year, the average tuition and fees were $8,000 for in-state students and $22,000 for out-of-state students.

Private schools are substantially more expensive. Add another $10,000 to $13,000 for room and board. If you live at home and attend an in-state school, your cost would be at the low end of $8,000 per year—or $32,000 for a four-year degree. If you attend an out-of-state school, you are looking at $32,000 to $35,000 per year—or $128,000 to $140,000 for a four-year degree.

If you choose to go to college, there are many universities and colleges with wonderful regional reputations, and a few with national and worldwide reputations, such as Harvard, Princeton, Yale, Brown, Cornell, Dartmouth, University of Pennsylvania, Georgetown, University of California Berkeley, and so on. Attending a school with a national or worldwide reputation has many advantages. With regionally well-known schools, the benefits of their reputation are regional. Therefore, if you attend an expensive school with a regional reputation in the northeast but do not plan to live in the northeast, you may be better off attending a school geographically closer to where you want to live. Unless you go to one of the top fifty schools in the nation, it doesn't make a whole lot of difference on your résumé.

It's very important to make sure the investment you make in your education is the right fit for your long-term goals and ability to pay off that debt.

Can't afford college? Research scholarships. Many scholarships and grant programs are available. A *short* listing of a Google search for available college scholarships follows:

- Minority students, first-generation students, international students, undocumented students, and students from various religious backgrounds
- Students from diverse backgrounds; full-ride scholarships, including leadership training and career development throughout college

- High-achieving, low-income students with full four-year scholarships
- High-achieving high school seniors with financial need who seek to attend and graduate from the nation's best four-year colleges and universities
- Achievement-based scholarships awarded to graduating high school seniors. Students are recognized for their capacity to lead, serve, and commit to making a significant impact on their schools and communities.
- Underserved Asian and Pacific Islander college students funds to support undergraduate education
- Outstanding minority high school seniors from low-income households. Top student leaders win a full-ride scholarship for their undergraduate studies.

Scholarship programs and grants range from hundreds to thousands of dollars, all the way to four-year scholarships. Good to know—right! Now, for the bad news: getting a scholarship sounds easy but is hard. Applying for a scholarship can be a long and tedious process. Similar to college applications, you will need to apply for several (maybe many) scholarships.

Where do you start? Again, I suggest your high school guidance counselor. He or she can provide guidance as to which colleges, community colleges, and scholarships to apply to and when to start the process. Sound like a lot of work? It is a lot of work and a big commitment as well, but it can pay off handsomely in the end. Many jobs require college degrees because of specific knowledge required, but many require the degree because it shows something about the individual—character, commitment to complete a difficult task, and so on—as well as broad-based education and maturity. Many of these qualities are required to complete the scholarship process. If you can't commit to the scholarship process, maybe college is not right for you (or maybe just not right now).

If you follow the scholarship path, maybe coupled with college loans, be sure to examine the complete financial picture and:

- Consider going to a community college for the first two years while living at home. The all-in cost of community college will save money over the cost of a four-year college.

- Prepare a budget of resources that include scholarships, loans, part-time jobs, and so on versus expenses, including tuition, books, room and board, and entertainment. If your projected expenses exceed your projected resources, adjustments are needed.

- Ensure that your major will result in a job with adequate income to support you and your loan payments.

If you finance your degree, it might take a long time—maybe decades—to pay off, especially if you land a low-level salaried or hourly job. Compare your anticipated salary to your total debt and look at the years it will take to pay off, but don't forget to consider your living expenses too.

What is left over after your living expenses, and what is available each month to pay against your college debt? The lender will treat your loan like any other lender does and expect consistent payments that take priority in your budget. And be aware that current bankruptcy law does not relieve student loan debt.

If your ideal career path won't support the cost of a college education, consider the alternative. There are many great jobs that do not require a college degree. There is a significant mismatch between available vocational and technical jobs versus available workforce. That means employers are having a difficult time finding skilled workers in the areas of manufacturing, transportation, construction, auto mechanics for high-end cars, and production of machines or tools. And many of these job opportunities pay more than jobs for college graduates, some paying six-figure wages.[1]

By planning ahead and leveraging all the tools and resources available, you can make a purposeful choice about your educational path that is more likely to serve you well long-term. Education is important for everyone, but this does not mean you need a four-year college degree. We currently have a national crisis of college graduates who are underemployed and cannot pay their college debt. You may be much better off with a marketable vocational or technical skill and without a large debt clouding your future.

---

1 Mitchell Schnurman, "Collin College's New Tech School Saves Time and Money, and Promises High-paying Jobs," Dallas Morning News, March 2020, https://www.dallasnews.com/business/jobs/2020/03/10/collin-colleges-new-tech-school-saves-time-and-money-and-promises-high-paying-jobs/.

Simply searching the internet will reveal a lot of information about jobs in demand that do not require a four-year degree. Some will require vocational or technical training, and some may require a two-year associate degree. Here are a few examples:

https://www.trade-schools.net/articles/
best-jobs-for-introverts

https://www.thebalancecareers.com/
best-trade-school-graduate-jobs-4125189

https://www.indeed.com/career-advice/
finding-a-job/highest-paying-trade-jobs

Nobody talks about forgiving trade-school debt because trade-school graduates can pay their own way. From the National Center for Construction Education & Research survey shown in the *Dallas Morning News*, the following list shows average annual salaries in 2018, not including overtime, per diem, or other incentives for a few trades that do not require a four-year degree:

Project Supervisor	$ 88,365
Combo Welder	$ 71,067
Instrumentation Tech	$ 70,080
Mobile Crane Operator	$ 66,119
HVAC Tech	$ 62,472
Commercial Electrician	$ 61,139

Plumber	$ 59,627
Commercial Carpenter	$ 56,877
Mason	$ 56,784

In the construction industry, just one out of ten workers is female. This represents an opportunity for women since some construction companies are aggressively recruiting and promoting women. This change in workplace culture has come about partly because of the labor shortage and partly to bring more diversity to corporate thinking and client interactions. In addition, it recognizes that women are significantly underrepresented. [2]

Women may be reluctant to enter construction because they're concerned about lifting building materials and handling heavy equipment. Others may be put off by the prospect of working in a male-dominated field.

But unlike in past decades, there are government rules and corporate policies to protect women, and good companies make sure female employees have a mentor to help navigate an unconventional workplace. Most women in the construction industry don't work on job sites. They're much more likely to be in an office setting, handling project estimates, design, human resources, and the like. They may not be building on-site, but they are building virtually.

According to an article in the *Dallas Morning News* written by Mitchel Schnurman, Collin College Technical Campus—just north of Dallas, TX—offers training,

---

2 Mitchell Schnurman, "Help Wanted: Why the Construction Industry Is Recruiting More Women," Dallas Morning News, March 2020, https://www.dallasnews.com/business/jobs/2020/03/06/help-wanted-why-the-construction-industry-is-recruiting-more-women.

certificates, and associate degrees in many specialized career paths, including carpentry, plumbing, automotive, electronics, welding, and a range of health sciences.

These so-called middle skills are in high demand and pay solid wages with the potential to reach six figures. Not only can earnings from these jobs actually rival—and sometimes exceed—the average pay for positions requiring a bachelor's degree, but these paths require just two years of postsecondary training and no student debt that follows one into the workplace.

Schnurman writes:

> The payoff? According to data compiled by Collin College, several jobs paid over $50,000 in average salaries in 2018. Construction managers earned six figures, and computer network support specialists were paid $80,000, the school said.
>
> A recent report from Georgetown University examined "the overlooked value of certificates and associate's degrees." About two million such credentials are awarded annually in the US, on par with the total number of bachelor's degrees.
>
> Depending on the specialty, some workers can earn more than those with a bachelor's degree, netting a higher return on their time, effort, and money.
>
> "As a result, less education can often be worth more," the report said.
>
> Other parts of the country are coming to the same conclusion as Collin College: That the middle-skills job sector is robust and growing and offers

a solid pathway to the middle class, said Anthony Carnevale, co-author of the Georgetown report.

"There's a message, especially to young people, that this is cool and necessary," said Carnevale, director of Georgetown's Center on Education and the Workforce. "And the community is willing to spend real money on it and give you first-class treatment."

Employers repeatedly told school leaders they wanted graduates to also have soft skills, especially in verbal and written communication. Collin College's associate's degree includes fifteen hours of core classes in humanities, English, communication and the like. [3]

There are significantly different college and career path options in demand and available today, so while this chapter does not seek to discourage anyone from pursuing a higher education, it does intend to broaden your perspective so you can choose wisely.

---

3   Mitchell Schnurman, "Collin College's New Tech School Saves Time and Money, and Promises High-Paying Jobs," Dallas Morning News, March 2020, https://www.dallasnews.com/business/jobs/2020/03/10/collin-colleges-new-tech-school-saves-time-and-money-and-promises-high-paying-jobs/.

MAPPING YOUR CAREER PATH

Going through life with a plan in mind is better than wandering aimlessly. And when you reach your destination, you don't want to have doubts about the journey and choices made or—more likely—choices *not* made. How can you possibly arrive at your desired destination without plotting your course?

A ship's helmsman navigates the course with a rudder. Individuals navigate their courses with life plans. Without a rudder, the helmsman has no control over direction, and without a plan, you have no control over your life's direction. Of course, as time passes, circumstances and the wind change; course corrections will be needed.

Some people have laser-guided focus on their career choices early on, but many do not. If you go to college, by the start of your third year, you should have a pretty good vision about how you will deploy your education in the career of your choice. The good news is that you don't have to figure it all out on your own. Seek out voices of experience to give you glimpses of possible future outcomes that you want to pursue or avoid.

Some people meandered into their careers or found their way serendipitously. If they had known then what they know now, would they have made different choices?

In many cases, yes.

Here are examples of major doubts many people have soon after starting their first real job:

- I should have majored in a discipline that was more marketable (i.e., will allow me to earn more money).

- I thought I would like working with young children.

- This job is tedious and boring.

- I shouldn't have settled for something I can do and instead trained for something I want to do.

If you have doubts like these, maybe you are headed in the right general direction, but your focus is slightly off. Accounting, finance, and business might have been the right general direction, but because of the many different flavors, maybe a midcareer course correction is needed. Maybe you prefer cost accounting over nonprofit accounting, banking over insurance, or auditing over posting accounting entries for a restaurant operator. The same can be true in most professions.

I knew an MD who did not like being a family doctor because many of his patients did not truthfully or accurately describe their symptoms. He then studied to become a dermatologist, thinking he would not depend on patients to describe their symptoms and could instead rely on his training to diagnose their particular skin condition. Then he found dermatology not to his liking, so after more years of a radiology residency, he found radiology to be the perfect choice. How nice that the search for the perfect specialty ended in success, but having not one but two false starts was costly in terms of medical school expenses and his time. Your goal should be to get your career choice right the first time.

Some people have a general idea of what they want to do (e.g., business management, accounting, finance, HR, taxes, teaching, medical, IT, and so on). But the more specific your goals, the less time you will waste figuring it out during your finite number of years in the workplace.

How do you select the best career path?

Here are several pointers to help you get started.

1. Take aptitude tests to identify your innate traits and abilities that most directly align with professionals in various careers. The results of aptitude tests will suggest a variety of fields and professions for you to consider. When you see the list, you may say, "That makes sense." Think of your relief when your inner self aligns with the aptitude results!

2. Talk to adults about their careers. This is an excellent opportunity to get an inside peek at a large number of professions. You are probably thinking:

    — I couldn't do that.

    — I'm too nervous.

    — When and where would I find these adults?

    — Why would they talk to me?

Many adults are looking for ways to engage with young people. You might start by talking to an adult at church or other social gatherings. Start with someone you know. Tell the person you are trying to decide on your career and ask if he or she would mind if you ask a few questions. Here are a few example questions:

- What do you do?
- What do you like/not like about your job?
- Do you think I might like _____?
- What courses should I take to prepare for a career in ____?
- Do you get to travel much? By yourself or with a team?

Once you break the ice, the conversation will flow easily, and the person may introduce you to other interesting adults.

3. Attend career fairs. College or high school meet-and-greets are great opportunities to speak with professors and alumni. Check with your guidance counselor at school about additional resources and venues and watch the local classified ads for job fair announcements.

When you do get that first job offer, remember to consider the entire offer. Money is just one component. Health care, hours, 401k, and things of that nature all need to be factored in. Comparing job offers depends on the individual. For some, a regular forty-hour workweek might be highly desirable, while others go for the money and don't mind working more hours. One size does not fit all.

After landing your first job, you may bounce around for a few years before finding your ideal work home. You can minimize this search period by understanding and purposefully using that information to stay on course in your career path. All work environments have different cultures and expectations, and you need to find the work culture that fits your personality best.

- Government work is policy- and procedure-based, is known to be stable, and generally offers a lifetime of employment, but some consider government work boring.

- Start-ups—young companies founded by one or more entrepreneurs—tend to be shoestring operations, meaning they are often not adequately financed and the concept has not been tested, which often results in failure. You will experience a lot of different activities and responsibilities that can be useful elsewhere, but start-ups are not known to offer long-term, stable employment.

- Turnarounds—companies that recover from losses and become profitable—are intense and risky. You will be exposed to myriad different activities and responsibilities, but the company has already demonstrated that long-term, stable employment may not be a reality.

- Small companies—meaning with fifty or fewer employees[4]—will provide exposure to many activities and responsibilities, along with a broader

---

4 http://www.oecd.org/.

awareness of how the company operates and profits. Growth opportunities are limited by the size of the organization, but you have the potential to be a big fish in a small pond. Small companies can feel more like a family, and this is something that you are unlikely to feel in a large company.

- Medium—midsize—companies, meaning with between fifty and two hundred and fifty employees, represent an averaging of the qualities of small and large companies.

- Large companies are those in manufacturing industries that employ five hundred or more individuals or those that do not manufacture goods but have an average of $7 million in annual receipts. You will most likely only see a small part of the organization's activities. There are many different ladders to climb, which creates opportunities for lateral moves on your way to the top, and lateral moves broaden your experience and make you more valuable to the organization. You might be a small fish in a large pond for your entire career, but you have the potential to be a big fish in a big pond. It is also worth noting that big organizations pay more for similar titles than small or medium companies and have excellent reputations for training employees in the latest IT systems and management techniques.

After gaining experience in a large organization, some people take their experience and move to small or medium organizations where their training is highly appreciated. After moving from a large to a small or medium organization, it is understood that moving back to a large organization is difficult. Large companies have infinitely more complex processes than small and medium organizations, and they tend to promote from within to leverage the training and development they endlessly provide. Once you leave that environment, the large company moves forward without you, continuously improving its technology, efficiency, and quality, such that you would no longer be "experienced" enough to pick up where you left off if you wanted to return.

Many new hires fail to correctly figure out a company's culture, resulting in leaving a position relatively quickly. Key indicators to research:

- Ask your recruiter why previous employees were successful.

- Ask your recruiter why other people left the company.

- While in the company's offices, notice whether employees smile at you or avoid eye contact. Pay attention to your sixth sense.

- Request a temporary contract position if you are unsure about your fit into the company's culture.

- Check out websites where employees leave employer reviews, basically explaining their experience while working for a company. Fairygodboss and Glassdoor are two good sites for this type of research.

Is it important to live in a big house with expensive luxury cars and a boat? If so, make sure the income potential of your career choice supports that lifestyle.

Earnings can differ greatly among college degrees. Science, technology, engineering, mathematics, and business can pay up to twice the salary of a liberal arts degree. Follow your dreams to the ideal career choice, but ensure you will be comfortable living the lifestyle your career provides.

Life's choices are about tradeoffs and balance. We all want to love our job and be excited about going to work. On the flip side, wouldn't it be terrible if we hated our job and had daily anxiety at the start of each day? Actual results will most likely be somewhere in the middle. Landing a job that you love is not an exact science. Like hand grenades and horseshoes, close may be good enough, and careful planning will certainly get you closer.

Also important, be wary of jumping between employers for a few more dollars because things aren't going right, or due to the influence of a recruiter. Too often employers see résumés of people who have flipped jobs every year or so, and, from their perspective, it is a real turn off. A good mentor may have perspective to help you analyze this important decision.

And finally, do not confuse a hobby with a vocation. We would all like to be able to make a living doing our hobby. Some of us can, but most can't and must search for a job that provides satisfaction and is enjoyable enough. Also remember that if you do pursue your hobby, you shouldn't expect to pursue it *like* a hobby. You'll have to work at it with a much greater level of intensity and responsibility. If you do pursue your hobby, be prepared for the possibility that it may end up not feeling like a hobby anymore.

"Learning how to think" really means learning how to exercise some control over how and what you think. It means being conscious and aware enough to choose what you pay attention to and to choose how you construct meaning from experience. Because if you cannot or will not exercise this kind of choice in adult life, you will be totally hosed.

—David Foster Wallace, writer and university professor (Kenyon College commencement speech, 2005)

MATCHING PERSONALITY TRAITS AND TALENTS TO CAREER

MAKING SURE YOUR PERSONALITY FITS into the demands of your career choice is an important exercise to help ensure your future success and comfort. One of the most popular and respected aptitude tests available is the Myers-Briggs Type Indicator (MBTI),[5] which is an introspective self-report questionnaire that indicates psychological preferences in how people make decisions and perceive the world. It is based on the belief that people experience the world using four principal psychological functions—sensation, intuition, feeling, and thinking—and that one of these four functions will be dominant most of the time. Identifying your natural tendencies will help you choose the right career path, and it will position you to enjoy your work and achieve the levels of success you desire.

Some may think that the above statements are a bunch of mumbo jumbo hokum. But consider this example: if you are an introvert and aspire for a career that is best suited for extroverts, you may be unhappy in your career choice. The MBTI will align your personality traits to a career choice that makes sense for you.

---

5 https://www.mbtionline.com/.

The MBTI aptitude test identifies four personality traits out of eight. You are either:

- **Extrovert (E) or Introvert (I)**
  Do you prefer to have a lot of social interaction and gain energy from staying busy and being in the company of many others? Or do you prefer to spend time alone or with just a small number of close friends or loved ones?

- **Sensing (S) or Intuition (N)**
  Do you most trust in what you can see, smell, hear, taste, or touch in the present moment, or do you use your intuition and trust your hunches first?

- **Thinking (T) or Feeling (F)**
  Do you place a high value on logic and consistent reasoning when making decisions? Or do you rely on feeling to consider the needs of everyone involved in a particular situation?

- **Judging (J) or Perceiving (P)**
  Do you prefer a lifestyle that looks fairly structured and routine? Are you orderly, disciplined, and less open to new information? Or do you have a preference for being spontaneous, adaptable, and open to new ideas and experiences?

The resulting four traits are arranged into sixteen

combinations of personality types.[6] For example, if you are an ESTJ—Extroverted, Sensing, Thinking, and Judging—the following is a sampling of professions that would be a good match for you.

- Business administrator
- Financial officer
- Government worker
- Insurance agent
- Judge
- Manager
- Military
- Nursing administrator
- Police/detective
- Sales representative
- Teacher
- Trade and technical
- Trade and technical teacher
- Underwriter

You will excel and become the best version of yourself when you take a strength-based approach to life.

---

6 See all sixteen combinations of personality types and the associated sampling of professions at https://www.iccb.org/iccb/wp-content/pdfs/adulted/tdl_bridge_curriculum/tdl_career_awareness/tdl_career_aware_resource_file/Suggested_Careers_for_MBTI.pdf.

Understanding your natural personality traits and making full use of that information is only part of the equation. Next, you should identify your natural talents and abilities.

To better understand your talents and maximize your potential, I recommend CliftonStrengths 34.[7] This resource helps you map out your complete unique talent DNA, providing interactive learning opportunities. It also provides a common language you can adopt for speaking about your strengths and weaknesses that is good for job interviews and career development discussions with mentors and/or employers.

In order to view a sample report of CliftonStrengths 34 results, go to:

> https://www.gallup.com/cliftonstrengths/
> en/253676/how-cliftonstrengths-works.aspx

and click "View Sample" toward the bottom of the page.

---

7   https://store.gallup.com/p/en-us/10003/cliftonstrengths-34.

MATCHING STRENGTHS AND INTERESTS TO CAREER

Each of us has academic strengths, hobbies, and passions. Let's call these strengths and interests the *Big Three*. Maybe your Big Three are talents or strengths you were born with that could be leveraged into an ideal career. In a perfect world, we would all choose a career that makes use of each of our strengths and interests. Too good to be true?

Let's take a look at some examples.

EXAMPLE 1

Academic strengths—math and physics

Hobbies—playing the saxophone and music in general

Passion—cars

Career target—industrial engineer for a car manufacturer, designing automobile sound systems

EXAMPLE 2

Academic strengths—business and industrial arts

Hobbies—water sports

Passion—fashion

Career target—swimwear prototype design/test market

EXAMPLE 3

Academic strengths—biology and chemistry

Hobbies—cooking

Passion—volunteering in a children's hospital

Career target—research on food allergies impacting children

The above examples were provided by Acceleron Learning, where the career targets were identified by using the following technique:

Looking at the above examples and knowing your Big Three, how easy would it be to identify the perfect career? It would probably not be easy. But if a third party were to think about your Big Three, they might make some useful recommendations. Better yet, if a group of five to ten people were to do the same exercise, great results are likely. So, consider testing the above exercise with your friends. Each person lists their Big Three—without identifying names—and the group suggests ideal career(s). You may have an aha moment. Go ahead and try it. I'll wait.

You've got to find what you love. And that is as true for your work as it is for your lovers. Your work is going to fill a large part of your life, and the only way to be truly satisfied is to do what you believe is great work. And the only way to do great work is to love what you do. If you haven't found it yet, keep looking. Don't settle....Your time is limited, so don't waste it living someone else's life. Don't let the noise of others' opinions drown out your own inner voice....And most importantly, have the courage to follow your heart and intuition.

—Steve Jobs, Apple cofounder (Stanford commencement address, 2005)

The website https://MyNextMove.org provides three approaches to help you decide what you want to do for a living:

- Answer questions about the type of work you might enjoy, and My Next Move will suggest careers that match your interests and training.
- Browse careers by industry. There are over nine hundred career options for you to view.
- Search careers with key words if you have some idea of you want to do.

HOURLY VS. SALARY MENTALITY

HOURLY EMPLOYEES ARE PAID FOR the time they work, with no exceptions. If you're in a well-compensated field with lots of overtime, you could make more than if you earned the same amount each pay period on a salaried basis. Hourly employees are also frequently able to achieve better work-life balance than salaried employees because their work schedules are generally fixed, with overtime often being an option. Salaried employees frequently must cancel plans at the end of their workday to get the job done on time.[8]

On the flip side, salaried employees will often have more or better benefit options (or both) and typically earn an overall higher income than hourly workers, while also enjoying the flexibility of being able to run personal errands during their shift without "clocking out" or using paid time off.[9] The ups and downs of any business will impact hourly employees more than salaried employees, as scheduled and overtime hours may be reduced while the salaried employees will receive the same paychecks regardless of the hours they work.

---

8   https://clockify.me/blog/business/salary-vs-hourly-employment/.

9   https://www.careerbuilder.com/advice/salary-or-hourly-wages.

If you are an hourly employee and aspire to be a salaried employee, better check to see if you have an hourly mentality in case you need to make some attitude adjustments.

Hourly mentality generalizations:
- It's only a job.
- Personal responsibilities are more important than career-pathing.
- You do not expect significant advancement or want additional responsibilities.
- Complaining to management about interpersonal issues isn't off-limits.
- You only owe the boss your scheduled shift.
- Work is drudgery, and it's impossible to get ahead.
- You could be fired at any time, for any reason, so you better sit down, shut up, and look busy.

Salaried/management generalizations:
- You view your job as a career.
- You are ambitious and will work more hours as the need arises.
- You want to move up in the organization and/or earn additional responsibilities.
- You carry more responsibility and stress.
- You make more money and have better benefits and job perks than hourly personnel.

Some people have an hourly mentality while others have a salaried mentality, and there is nothing wrong with either configuration. Both hourly and salaried employees have reasons for their choices, like the hourly employee who may require a more stable schedule for such reasons as child or senior care, night school, and so on. All companies need a combination of both, and your respective attitude to hourly versus salary should ensure that you are drawn to the best fit for you.

Salaried employees often have an ambitious appetite for advancement in responsibilities and salary. I had a boss who informed me that the average work week for salaried staff was fifty hours, but there would be times when I would be required to flex up and work more. And he did not disappoint. I had a heavy workload and many special projects. If your career path is meant to take you into management and you think you are going to get ahead by working forty hours per week, you're wrong!

The point is that you need to recognize there is a difference between the hourly and salaried mentality and decide which is right for you. And your choice may change over time, so being aware of the pros and cons for both options in your field or company or both will come in handy as life changes.

Whether you are an hourly or salaried employee, advancement opportunities come up from time to time, and senior management decides who gets the promotion. If you want to be on the salaried/management track but demonstrate an hourly mentality to your supervisor, you may not be considered. If you are new to the world of work, you may not understand why Jane got the promotion instead of you. If this is so, it's time for some self-examination. Additionally, this is one of those issues to discuss with your mentor. If you understand what qualities senior management is looking for, you are in a better position to prepare to be selected for the next open position.

SALARY, WAGES, COMPENSATION, AND YOUR MAJOR AND YOUR COLLEGE

Some people are motivated by money and some are not, but we all have bills to pay and a vision of a lifestyle that we want now and in the future. It is important for students to follow their passions, but remember if you choose a high-priced major in a low-paying field, you may be paying for your college education over many years.

Average salaries and the market demand for various majors are available on the web, but students do not seem to be taking advantage of this information. The University of Texas teamed up with the Census Bureau to show how much money graduates earn, broken down by major and campus. The idea was to help students make good choices. If they knew that one major resulted in a higher salary than others—or that graduates from one university earn more than those with the exact same degree from another—wouldn't they make the higher-paying choice? Two years after the groundbreaking collaboration began, students have not seemed to alter course, said David Troutman, the system's associate vice chancellor, who oversees the project.

That students do not know their likely future incomes

long before they graduate is particularly surprising given that getting a good job is now the number one reason students go to college. Knowing the long-term financial returns of a college education is more than picking the most lucrative major. It's also about knowing whether money borrowed for an education could exceed the income from a job to which it leads.

College loan debt is a serious issue for many college graduates as well as our country. The long-term debt of nearly $1.6 trillion exceeds accumulated car loans and even credit card debt. By almost any definition, this is a *crisis:* It is certainly a crisis for those with student loan debts whose repayment schedules span decades, with large monthly payments. It is also a crisis for lenders experiencing significant default rates. This debt has been fueled by decades of wages not keeping up with the rising cost of college as well as students chasing expensive degrees with low wages.

Texas legislators have required that the online form used by applicants for Texas public universities include prominent links to employment rates and some wage information. Many states have similar requirements. The Texas pilot program is being copied in Colorado, Michigan, New York, Pennsylvania, and Wisconsin. Before selecting a college and a major, you should avail yourself of this information.[10]

---

10 Jon Marcus, "Data on Well-Paying Majors not Swaying Students—Yet," Dallas Morning News, Dec, 27, 2010, https://edition.pagesuite.com/popovers/dynamic_article_popover.aspx?artguid=bb4fefae-bef1-4ca3-8248-5af073d0815c&appid=3565.

SUMMER JOBS

Summer jobs provide a variety of benefits to high school kids, college kids, and parents/grands/mentors. For my generation, summer jobs helped us identify what we liked and did not like about a specific job or industry and also provided spending money. For those of us who did not like entry-level jobs, it gave us an incentive to study and work hard for our college degree.

In addition, each summer job provided a window into the work environment and what it was like to report to a boss. Many of our bosses were the same age as we were or close to our age. Most of these young bosses were inexperienced and did not have the benefit of management training and therefore made rookie mistakes. These rookie mistakes were hard on us, sometimes arbitrary and mean-spirited, but ultimately benefited us by making us stronger, more resilient, and tough.

In addition, we learned what not to do when we were promoted or assigned to a management position with personnel responsibilities. Let's look at some summer job experiences as well as a couple of new employee experiences.

Before we proceed, please note that only difficult situations are being discussed because that is where you maximize your experience and learning about the world of work. These experiences will benefit you in the future. But do not assume that work is full of nothing but bad situations. There are plenty of good things that happen in the world of work, including

- earning money to buy those things you want or need;
- meeting new people and making friends;
- working as a team and the camaraderie that comes with completing an assigned task;
- getting compliments on a job well done;
- learning how things are done, including procedures, paperwork, and customer service in a variety of industries;
- progressing beyond your first day when you are scared and nervous to a short time later when you have confidence in your ability to do the job better and better;
- feeling that you are making a contribution to the organization and are appreciated;
- building your self-confidence and feelings of accomplishment; and
- knowing that your summer job is just that, and any rookie mistakes made will not go on your "permanent record."

Sears—Candy Counter—A friend of mine was in the loss prevention department at his local Sears store. A young employee in the candy department was on the pudgy side and seemed always to be eating something. So my friend assumed that she was helping herself to the company's candy. Not knowing how to address this situation and not having any supervisory training, he decided to weigh this young woman and everybody else in the department at the start and end of the shift. Any weight gain would indicate candy theft and would result in termination of the offending candy employee. My friend was proud of himself for devising such a clever plan, and his immediate supervisor was also supportive of this new and proactive procedure to control theft. Really? Can you believe that this actually happened? My friend should have been the one who was terminated. Of course, this highly offensive and illegal practice was discontinued after a seasoned manager became aware of the situation.[11]

Was there a better way to handle this situation? Of course, there was. There should have been face-to-face conversation to reiterate that candy department protocol stated that employees were not to eat company candy without first paying for it and further, employees were not to eat while on duty.

There are at least two or three takeaways from the above situation.

- Ask for help on how to address a particular problem, particularly if you are unsure of how to handle it. My friend should have felt unsure about the practice of weighing in. If he had been a little

---

11 Carlos Merla, Core Events of Cultural Awareness: Fiction and Nonfiction Tales of Cultural Competency and a Proud Latino Heritage (2016), 35.

older when this happened, his actions could have been a career-limiting event.

- Develop the skills to have uncomfortable-face-to-face conversations. You will need to be honest, straightforward, but not unkind. Focus on the actions and/or behavior, but do not get personal. As a manager, you will have regular face-to-face conversations with your employees for performance reviews and corrective action conversations. It is important to become proficient at these situations. These skills will also come in handy when you need to have a difficult conversation with many types of individuals—your boss, peers, customers, or vendors.

- Today's employees are more insulated from the actions of bad managers than in the 1960s and prior. If this situation occurred today, you would be well within your rights to present the weigh-in/weigh-out procedure to HR in a professional manner, without outrage and attitude, and let HR handle it.

Before we continue, let's talk about the role of HR. HR's primary responsibility and obligation is to the company. If you take an issue to HR like the one we are discussing, HR will view the issue as it relates to the company (e.g., is the company exposed if they do nothing?). HR is primarily there to protect the company from lawsuits, and if you benefit from their actions, so much the better. For more information on HR, see chapter "Navigating Corporate America III."

When filing a complaint with HR, many times, an employee will hold to a principle and win the battle but lose the war. Although it shouldn't happen this way, sometimes a complaint can backfire and negatively impact your career path. So, be cautious about how important that complaint is to you.

There are some tough and demanding bosses out there, and many of these bosses are at the top of the totem pole. One new district manager (DM) hired for a multiunit retail operation tells the following story. His first day on the job was at the DM's meeting where he would meet his management team and introduce himself. After the preliminaries were done, the CEO quietly told the new DM he wanted him to fire one of his managers. The conversation went something like this.

DM—OK, I will evaluate the talent in my district and make a decision.

CEO—You don't understand; they are all bad. It doesn't matter whom you fire. Pick one during the next session that you lead, fire him, and send him home now.

NOTE—The CEO wanted to get his bluff in on the DM, and he also wanted the new DM to get his bluff in on his management team (i.e., to put fear into the management team). This management style was the tone from the top and not surprising; nobody liked the CEO. In spite of this tone, the employees pulled together as a team to support each other. Amazingly, it worked, and the company grew dramatically and made the CEO rich beyond belief.

You might think that this company would have a hard time finding and keeping employees. To my surprise, this was not the case.

- Is this type of management style illegal? No.
- Is it harsh? Definitely.
- Is it effective? It can be.

This type of harsh management style from the top works best if middle management converts it into a productive influence, rather than sending fear down the ranks. For example: A VP of warehouse operation had an office on the warehouse floor with floor to ceiling windows on three sides. The CEO would often visit the VP of warehouse operations and chew him out in an animated fashion. When the CEO left the VP's office, one might expect the VP to go to the warehouse floor and chew out his people. Instead, he would go to the warehouse floor and talk to several employees who witnessed the incident. The VP would greet the employees and maybe ask about a family member and then ask about a warehouse issue. His employees were bowled over by his ability to be civil to them after being chewed out by the big boss. By word of mouth, these stories eventually made it to everyone in the warehouse, and the VP of operations was truly loved and respected because he did not send fear down the ranks. His employees would do anything for this man.

Periodically, our buckets get full, and it is tempting to dump on a subordinate. Don't do it or rarely do it and you will be rewarded with respect as well as a staff that will follow and support you.

And finally, how does this impact you, and how can you avoid working for a company like this? As mentioned in the "Mapping Your Career Path" chapter, when in the company's office for an interview, pay attention to your sixth sense. Do the employees smile at you or avoid eye contact? Do the employees appear happy? Check out websites where employees leave employer reviews, basically explaining their experience while working for a company. Fairygodboss and Glassdoor are two good sites for this type of research.

Payroll Dollars—The two biggest expenses in restaurant and retail businesses and many other businesses are payroll and product cost. For some businesses, payroll cost is the biggest expense item. Local, district, regional and corporate management look at these two line items and put immense pressure on management at all levels to bring this cost down. Below is an example of questionable/illegal tactics to reduce payroll costs.

My first job was at a burger joint, and my hourly wage was $1.60 per hour. That was the going wage back then, and I was happy to get a paycheck, especially my first paycheck. Teens below the age of eighteen were not allowed to work past midnight. If our location closed late due to customer demand, we were often not able to clean the location before midnight. Management's solution was to not pay the underage teens for work done after midnight. This was wrong and illegal, but to reduce payroll cost, it happened. This action could have exposed the company and the manager to the federal Wage and Hour Division's enforcement. As a teen employee, I would have probably won, and local news reporting on this violation would not have been good for the local burger joint.

Looking back on this issue, I have mixed emotions about having kept quiet. Standing up to management would have earned me a few extra bucks, but while the case with the federal Wage and Hour Division's ground on, the burger joint would not have been able to schedule hours for me. Even if the burger joint had scheduled me, the environment would have been toxic. In addition, the news reporting of this situation would have ensured I did not land a replacement summer job. Looking back, I probably did the most expeditious thing, but to this day, this injustice still bothers me.

In your summer jobs, and probably beyond, you will undoubtedly encounter situations that are not right or may be borderline. How you address these situations is up to you, but be assured there are consequences. Please know that you are not the first to experience these types of injustices.

Some of these injustices are small, but some can be large. You need to ask yourself if your particular injustice is worth going to battle. Or to put it another way, "Is the juice worth the squeeze?" I have been behind closed doors on numerous occasions where employees who complain were labeled as troublemakers, and the department head or even the CEO or president would say something to the effect of, "OK, they got us this time, but I want her supervisor to grind her out. I do not want her to be here by the end of next quarter." Senior management applies pressure to the manager to find a way to terminate a "troublemaker." So, a word to the wise: Don't be a troublemaker, and don't be trouble for your immediate supervisor, your supervisor's boss, or the boss's boss. Adapt and be a problem solver instead.

Flipping burgers—one additional story—When you are the new guy, you are going to be asked to do the most undesirable tasks. In addition, you are probably going to be razzed and pranked, so just expect it. I don't remember all of the pranks, but there were more than a few. Since I was new to the working world and the fast-food business, sometimes it was hard to tell what was real and what was "a snipe hunt."

After working what I thought were all the burger positions, I was asked to clean the grease trap. This was a vile, disgusting, and smelly job, and I was not really sure that it was for real. After all, doesn't the grease drain into the grease trap to be picked up by a grease truck? After being pranked, I was not sure this was a real job, so I refused to do the task.

Turns out, it was a real job, and my hours were cut for not performing this task. To this day, I regret not cleaning the grease trap. Looking back, I should have asked some questions to gain a better understanding, but I was young and inexperienced and made a mistake.

Probably a better approach would have been to say to my boss, "As a new guy on the team, I have been asked to do a number of things that were not real job-related tasks. That is, I have been pranked. So, before I start this task, I want to be certain it is a real job that needs to be done."

Camp counselor—The summer before I attended SMU studying for an MBA, I worked as a camp counselor. The camp was large, fifty cabins with ten campers per cabin and two counselors per cabin. There were two five-week overnight sessions and a large staff to watch over the campers and camp counselors.

Most of the staff who supervised the counselors were awesome, but there were a few bad apples in the crowd. I remember one supervisor who was a jerk. I guess the power of his position had gone to his head. Maybe he had been breathing his own exhaust too long.

When camp was over for the season, I drove to Dallas to start an MBA program, and to my surprise, this particular camp supervisor was in my class. The first two days of class typically start with each of the professors telling students how hard the program is and how hard we are going to work if we want to graduate. As the two first days progressed, I was in contact with my camp supervisor, and he was struggling with what the professors told us as well as the homework assignments. At the end of the first two days, he dropped out, telling me that he would not survive the curriculum. I tried to talk him out of quitting, but to no avail.

The takeaway here appears to be that I was not scared off by the revelation of hard work; I expected it. My camp supervisor was not mentally tough, nor did he have the confidence to persevere even though he had survived the admission process. So although many summer jobs have uncomfortable situations, they prepare us in ways that we do not expect for the future. These jobs toughen us up and make future difficulties a nonevent. Had that counselor not been too busy being a know-it-all jerk, he might have learned what he would need to be successful in college.

Waiting tables—No discussion of summer jobs would be complete without talking about waiting tables. If you have waited tables, you probably have stories about unreasonable or pain-in-the-ass (PITA) customers. And when you go out to eat, you probably are more forgiving to your waitstaff than the general public. Maybe you've wondered why you can't land a job in a nicer restaurant where the cost of a meal is higher, the resulting tips are higher, and servers have fewer tables to serve.

With experience and attention to some of the customers' pet peeves rather than taking it personal and letting a negative perspective of their behavior impede your open-minded efforts to learn, you will have an opportunity to land a job in a nicer restaurant, where servers can make into the six figures. As a customer, some pet peeves include the following:

- Eye contact ignored—A customer needs something and cannot find the server. Maybe the server is in the area but ignores the customer's attempt to get attention.

- Interruptions—You are telling your tablemates a story and are one line away from the punch line, and your server asks, "How is everything?" Or maybe it is a business lunch and your server interrupts an important conversation.

- Food is delivered, but you have no silverware

- Drink is empty—Never let a customer's drink glass be more than one-third empty, particularly if it is an alcoholic beverage. That will increase your opportunity for a larger tip.

- Check not delivered when the meal is complete—After the meal is complete and the customer needs to go back to work, the server is missing in action.

- Tablemates are not served at the same time—Polite company waits for everybody to be served before eating. So while you are waiting for everybody to be served, your food is getting cold.

- Asking if you are ready to order when everyone at the table is obviously still reading the menu—Might be better to say, "I will come back after you have had a chance to read the menu." When the menus are down and everybody is ready to order, the server is nowhere in sight.

- Order is incorrect.

In my humble opinion, after you master all of the basics of being a server, the single most important thing you can do to improve yourself so that you land a high-paying server job is to *learn to read the table*. That is, to determine the specific needs of your table through observation. Are they there to celebrate, for business, or there just for a meal? Are they on a first date or in a long-term relationship? Do they have a lively conversation that should not be interrupted or are they looking to interact with their server? Are they high- or low-maintenance customers?

In my experience as a customer, the best service comes at the nicer restaurants. These servers have experience, and it shows. An executive from one of my former employers tells a story about the exceptional service received at a lunch meeting. After being seated, their server brought water and asked if anyone would like anything else to drink. When asked if the group would like to hear the specials, the server was told that they needed to discuss some business, and they would let him know when they were ready to order. The server did not disturb them but was sufficiently vigilant about paying attention to be there when they were ready to order.

When the group was ready, the server was there in an instant. The first lady liked the looks of the dinner salad at the next table but only wanted half the serving plus six crisp French fries. That's right: six crisp French fries. The second gentleman requested special preparation due to dietary preferences. The third gentleman wanted to taste two entrées before making his selection. The fourth lady ordered off the menu, but with a couple of substitutions.

As each order was placed, the server said, "Yes, sir," or "Yes, ma'am." By reading the table, the server knew that he did not need to say anything about the special pricing of their orders. After the taste was done and the third gentleman placed his order, all orders were turned in to the kitchen.

The kitchen used a computer system that indicated when to start each order so that everything was ready at the same time. When the food was brought to the table, there were two servers so that all plates were placed at the same time. In addition, the servers knew who was to receive each meal—there was no food auction, that is, *Who got the salad? Who got the French fries?* and so on. The meal was so perfect that this story has been told many times.

Normally, the opposite occurs. If the service is bad, guests tell everybody they run across. But in this case, the food and service were exceptional, the server received a large tip, and the restaurant guests recommended both the restaurant and the server to their business associates and family and friends. That server not only did a great job of serving the guests, but also was credited with bringing in additional customers. Very cool!

Could the above experience happen at Chili's? Probably not, but this example may help you raise your serving standards to the next level.

Working with the public, you will see a mix of humanity—the good, the bad, and the ugly of people. As you move through life, whether working with the public or not, you will continue to see the good, bad, and ugly in people. These views will provide insight into how others see you in various situations and provide an opportunity for you to change your behavior in order to be the person you want to be. I hope you strive to be one of the good in all that you do and say.

Summer jobs and résumés—When applying for your first permanent job, list the jobs you held while in school on your résumé, even if it was flipping hamburgers at McDonald's or mowing lawns. It shows initiative and willingness to work.

PART II
GETTING AND KEEPING A JOB

INTEGRITY

Don't cheat, steal, lie, or do anything you would not want your mother reading or hearing about on the news or internet. Your integrity is more important than a test grade or a falsified résumé, and the consequences of poor integrity are costly and have long-term consequences. Being of high moral character and having integrity also means doing the right thing when no one is watching.

When we are children, we first learn to get our way by crying or throwing a temper tantrum. As we grow older, we find that temper tantrums won't bring the desired results. Maybe our next strategy is to sneak a treat after a parent has said no, and then we learn about the consequences of that bad behavior. As we mature from childhood to adolescence to adulthood, most of us develop a moral compass and do the right thing because we want to feel good about ourselves. We develop integrity.

But not everybody takes the high road. Have you ever done any of the following?

- Stolen anything?
- Cheated on a test?
- Borrowed money, a computer, iPad, tools, or books from a friend and not returned them?

- Cheated on your expense report?
- Not returned a library book?
- Frequently forgotten your wallet when going out with friends?
- Underpaid when the restaurant bill was split?

If you answered yes to three or more of these questions, you are headed down the wrong path and are drifting in the wrong direction. Maybe you have drift disease and are on the path to the dark side. Whether you've strayed or just not thought about being the kind of professional that will ensure you achieve your career goals, this chapter will help with self-examination so you can make the necessary changes.

It's not new or uncommon that average Joes and Janes commit various types of theft in the workplace. Surprisingly, there is also a long list of companies defrauded by senior executives who were ultimately responsible for protecting the company's and shareholders' assets. A small sampling of thefts and bad behavior and the resulting punishment follow.

- A falsified résumé discovered after hiring resulted in termination and a "not subject to rehire" on the company's records. Future employment verification resulted in a no-hire by future companies.

- A salesclerk used sales receipts that customers left behind to refund merchandise for cash. This clerk was caught and criminally charged with fraud.

- An administrative worker set up bogus companies and submitted invoices to his employer for payment. This former worker is serving a prison sentence.

- Actress Felicity Huffman is a Primetime Emmy Award winner, a Golden Globe Award winner, and winner of three Screen Actors Guild Awards. She has received nominations for an Academy Award and a BAFTA Award. Felicity is also a convicted felon. She was one of fifteen parents who pled guilty on a conspiracy-related fraud charge in the college-admission cheating scheme. She was convicted and sentenced to fourteen days in prison, two hundred and fifty hours of community service, a $30,000 fine, and one year of supervised release. In addition, she appears to now be estranged from the daughter she was trying to help get into college.[12]

- Accountant Sandy Jenkins was sentenced to ten years in federal prison for fleecing Collin Street Bakery of nearly $16 million. Sandy was sixty-six at the time.[13]

- Dubious accounting practices resulted in the bankruptcy of Enron, a US energy commodities and service company. Enron valued at more than

---

12 Melissa Korn and Jennifer Levitz, "Huffman Sentenced to 14 Days," Wall Street Journal, September 14–15, 2019.

13 Federal Bureau of Investigation, "Former Collin Street Bakery Executive and Wife Sentenced," September 16, 2015. www.fbi.gov/contact-us/field-offices/dallas/news/press-releases/former-collin-street-bakery-executive-and-wife-sentenced .

$60 billion in assets and was involved in one of the biggest bankruptcy filings in the history of the United States. Many top executives were charged with fraud, the harshest sentence going to CEO Jeffrey Skilling, who received a twenty-four-year sentence and was required to give $42 million to the victims of the Enron fraud.[14]

- A Ponzi scheme orchestrated by Bernie Madoff produced a loss estimated at $64.8 billion. Bernie, former chairman of the NASDAQ stock market, was sentenced to one hundred and fifty years in prison.[15]

Justification for such actions comes in many forms:

- To get the job
- To get into an Ivy League school
- To relieve debt—likely resulting from living beyond one's means
- To have lots of big presents under the Christmas tree
- To pay large medical expenses
- To fund an extravagant lifestyle

---

14 Juan A. Lozano, "Former Enron CEO Skilling Sentenced to 24 Years," Seattle Times, October 23, 2006, www.seattletimes.com/business/former-enron-ceo-skilling-sentenced-to-24-years/.

15 Chase Peterson-Withorn, "The Investors Who Had to Pay Back Billions in Ill-Gotten Gains from Bernie Madoff's Ponzi Scheme," Forbes, April 14, 2021, www.forbes.com/sites/chasewithorn/2021/04/14/the-investors-who-had-to-pay-back-billions-in-ill-gotten-gains-from-bernie-madoffs-ponzi-scheme/?sh=175aa20b64ed.

- To stroke one's ego—more is better
- To record fraudulent accounting entries at the request of senior management.

The common denominator is that the above individuals did not have high moral character, and all found a way to rationalize that their behavior was okay. Did they think about their parents or family and friends reading or hearing in the news or internet about their actions? Did they think about the resulting dire consequences for themselves, their family, company employees—who lost both their jobs and their company retirement monies? Did these thieves have drift disease, where their misdeeds started with the minor theft of a candy bar, which gradually increased in size sufficient to bring down a multibillion-dollar company? Or was their need so great? Or maybe they were locked into future improprieties once they made the first improper accounting entry at the request of senior management.

The answer to why these bad guys did what they did could be any of the above and many more, but there is no excuse for lack of integrity. This position is supported by the judiciary system, which has no sympathy for thefts and frauds. If you have integrity and do the right thing when no one is watching, you will never lose sleep over worrying when the authorities will come for you.

Many companies have both a loss prevention department and an internal audit department. These two departments work on a basic premise that:

- Some people never steal.
- Some people always steal.

- The vast majority won't steal if they think they're going to get caught.

With this in mind, loss prevention and internal audit departments put policies and procedures in place—internal controls—to ensure that employee and customer theft does not occur. If theft does occur, the procedures will identify the theft for investigation. The message is: Don't think you won't get caught.

Some companies have zero tolerance for theft. Early in my career, I witnessed a pharmacist being terminated for stealing a magazine. That seemed a little harsh at the time. I later learned that this pharmacist had been stealing both cash and medications, but the theft of the magazine was the only item that could be proven. Another company that had hundreds of retail shops, many run by young women, posted in the monthly newsletter an animated picture of a young woman behind bars with the following caption: Who will raise your kids while you are in jail?

Effective?

I think so!

DO THE RIGHT THING

If you are leading a team and make poor ethical or strategic decisions—or focus on money or power versus what is right—you can destroy your group's willingness to follow you.

Examples:

- A large retail company held a much-anticipated annual warehouse sample sale for its employees until one employee complained about the order in which employee groups were allowed to enter the sale. The CEO decided the solution was to discontinue the employee sales. The same company had two Christmas parties each year, one for the kids and one for the adults. The underprivileged upbringing of the company's founder was the genesis of this generous practice. Because one employee complained that it was unfair since employees with kids received benefits and those without kids did not, the CEO canceled the kids' Christmas party. These two decisions were part of a trend in which the CEO did not do the right thing, and as a result, this CEO lost the support of the management team, the employees, and the board.

- I heard a story about a business coach hired to improve an executive's management skills. On the first day, the coach heard the executive speak to a group of managers, sharing a story he'd heard on a nature show the previous weekend. A sick elephant was down, and the other elephants gathered around to protect the sick one and put sand on him to protect him from the sun. The second segment was about penguins. One was sick, and the others gathered around and pecked him to death. Then the executive asked, "What are we?" After a moment, he said, "We are tough like penguins!" The business coach said that you could have heard a pin drop as people in the room were mentally updating their résumés. This company is no longer in business.

Always consider how your decisions and remarks will be received by others as well as how your remarks and decisions will impact how others perceive you. Both the golden rule and the platinum rule should be part of your foundation no matter what role you play. This is especially true for anyone aiming toward leadership roles.

- Golden Rule—Do unto others as you would have them do unto you.
- Platinum Rule—Do unto others as they would have you do unto them.

While always doing the right thing, be sure to avoid saying the wrong thing. David Hayden, restaurant consultant, lends the following advice. Many restaurant supervisors and managers are promoted from the hourly restaurant pool due to their experience and hard work. However, their management experience has not been tested. Their management skills have to be developed by trial and error with some help from their supervisors. If you are a fast starter and upwardly mobile, you might find yourself in a management role much faster than you expect. The following are three things that should not be said by managers of any experience level.

"THIS IS A DICTATORSHIP, NOT A DEMOCRACY."

No one disputes the validity of this statement. The manager is there to make decisions and run the show. A business should not be a democracy. At the same time, there are more appropriate ways to state it than in such an uncaring way to the staff. Most dictatorships end in revolutions or coups, with the dictator facing a firing squad. If you refuse to give your staff a voice, they will still speak out behind your back. This is devastating for morale and can spread rapidly. Dictators must live in a state of paranoia, as everyone under their rule is looking for a chance to put a knife in their back.

"IT'S NOT MY DECISION."

This is the converse of the mentality above. Rather than ruling with an iron fist, these sorts of managers avoid any responsibility. They are content to blame their boss, the company, and so on to avoid being the one to upset their staff. The most immediate consequence is for the staff to continue complaining about the decision. Whatever hostility was generated by the decision is made worse because now, not even the manager supports it. When a manager denies accountability in this way, it becomes tougher for the person to enforce accountability in his or her staff. While this is generally done to maintain staff, it usually has the opposite effect. Managers who cannot stand up for a decision actually marginalize themselves by sending the message that they are not really in charge.

"DO AS I SAY, NOT AS I DO."

This is by far the most damaging of the three. You will notice each of these three statements is slightly patronizing. All are things you would say to a petulant child. This one makes it clear that a double standard exists. Managers who use this method are really sending a clear message to their staff that they think they are superior. The same rules do not apply because they are in charge. This first calls the validity of the rule into question and then forces the staff to respond in kind. If the staff are treated like children, they will respond in childish ways. When managers consistently engage in activities that they discipline hourly employees for doing, they are creating an atmosphere that kills morale.

It is never easy to motivate employees. In addition, the above mistakes can quickly kill motivation and breed revolution. So much of a manager's success is based upon the work of staff. No manager can do everything it takes to run a successful business on his or her own. It takes a team for a business to succeed. A manager's job is to inspire the best performance possible from a team. When managers fail to do so, the results can range from failure to sabotage to a coup. Leading staff through motivation is not easy, but it is vital.

TWO WOLVES

The story of two wolves is a popular legend of unknown origin, sometimes attributed to the Cherokee or Lenape people.

Grandfather tells this metaphorical story to his grandchild:

There are two wolves inside us, fighting for supremacy.

One wolf represents one or more of anger, envy, greed, fear, lies, insecurity, ego, darkness, despair, hate, evil, and sin.

The other represents peace, love, compassion, kindness, humility, positivity light, hope, righteousness, and goodness.

The grandchild asks which wolf wins. Grandfather says it will be the one you feed.

We feed the wolf with:

- What we read and hear
- Whom we spend time with
- What we do with our time
- Where we focus our energy and attention.

Every choice in life is a battle between two wolves inside us.

Choose wisely!

DIGITAL MANNERS

Elements of a good email, according to the Emily Post Institute's Daniel Post Senning in an article in the *Wall Street Journal*:

- Craft a clear subject line. This is an increasingly important digital courtesy in an age of overstuffed inboxes, as the subject line can help people sort, tag, and find the email later.

- Use proper salutations and closings. This helps to set the tone for communication.

- Don't include text-speak. Avoid abbreviations and emoji in emails.

- Minimize the use of exclamation points.

- Don't write in all capital letters.

The above might seem obvious, but here is an example of a common problem. An eighth grader sends an email to his teacher that reads, "Hey, can you send me that paper?" With no subject line, no signature, and only a portion of the student's name, the teacher is left to piece together the sender and which paper the student is requesting. This situation provided an excellent example for the teacher to use as a teaching moment.[16]

The issue is that people tend to think selfishly in little ways like this, assuming what they want to say is all someone needs. Digital communication doesn't automatically bring a name and a face and doesn't automatically pinpoint the one out of hundreds of other things something could be. We need to remember to view digital communication from the other person's perspective so that we provided sufficient information and background to allow the addressee to respond to our email without follow-up questions. You might ask a friend for "that paper," and they'll know you mean the one you were working on earlier that day, but if you ask a manager of a department, there may be a lot more to consider when any one of the team members in that department is vague.

Texting may be second nature to many kids, but composing an email seems like an ancient craft. That's so last century. But email is still the number one form of communication in the workplace and very important for college and career readiness.

With that said, it is still important to consider generational issues when choosing a digital method of communication. Younger counterparts may prefer texting, while colleagues may prefer email. Think about the age of the recipient and the person's preferred form

---

16   Julie Jargon, "Mind those Manners: Kids Need Lessons in Email and Phone Etiquette: When It Comes to Making Calls and Composing Messages, a Lack of Social Graces Isn't Something to LOL about," Wall Street Journal, Feb. 11, 2020, https://www.wsj.com/articles/mind-those-manners-kids-need-lessons-in-email-and-phone-etiquette-11581417001.

of communication—email, text, phone, or other—while deciding the best way to get your message across.

In written composition, tone conveys the attitude of a writer toward a subject or an audience. Tone is generally communicated through word choice and the viewpoint a writer takes on a particular subject. Every written piece comprises a central theme or subject matter, and the way a writer approaches this theme or subject is the person's tone. Examples of literary tone are airy, comic, condescending, funny, heavy, intimate, playful, sad, sinister, serious, solemn, angry, or threatening.

After you compose your email, reread your composition for spelling errors, punctuation issues, and proper tone. You might ask yourself if—in your judgment—the recipient will read your email with the intended tone. Use the spelling and grammar checker for all email, Word, and Excel documents. You may learn grammar along the way, such as when to use "who" versus "whom" or "its" versus "it's" and a lot more.

Never send an angry email, text, or post. A gym buddy told me about an unfortunate anger email issue at his office. Payroll checks over the Thanksgiving holiday were to be issued on the Monday after Thanksgiving, rather than the usual Friday. Although the payroll check schedule was publicized a year in advance, one of the engineers was furious about the timing difference. As a result, this engineer composed a ranting email in all caps and sent it to all employees of the company.

If you are angry, it is okay to write the email, but wait a few hours to see if you still want to hit the send button. This engineer immediately hit the send button, and soon after, he was terminated and escorted from the building. The engineer's personnel records probably indicate "not eligible for rehire." We all write angry emails or texts from time to time, but everyone feels different after taking time to calm down from the initial reaction. Remember to act instead of react. Vent to your keyboard, then wait to be sure you really want to publicize that reaction or revise your approach to take a more appropriate—and more likely to be successful—action.

Your tone is not always easy to gauge in writing because the body language part of face-to-face communication is not present. Word choices—combined with aesthetics like properly capitalized and punctuated sentences versus all caps and sloppy writing—will replace those visual clues. Will the recipient read your email with your intended tone? If, after rereading your email and waiting before hitting the send button, you are still uncertain about the tone, listen to your sixth sense and do not send until you are no longer uncertain.

If you are working on an email where you are pitching a point, trying to convince your reader to do something or writing about an issue that has a number of moving parts, it is often best to let the email marinate in your head before sending. After your first draft, reread your email, say, thirty minutes later, and you will most likely see points to add and better ways organize and overall improve your first draft. It is probably best to repeat this exercise until no changes are made after rereading. This approach will help ensure that you do not send one or more follow up emails with things you forgot to include or clarification of convoluted wording. Getting emails right the first time will make you look like a pro. This includes attaching the file you referred to in the body of your email before sending it out, which is actually one of the more common mistakes made in emails, to forget the attachment. Consider attaching the file first, before composing the email. If you change the attachment before sending the email, don't forget to delete and reattach the file.

SEX, RELIGION, AND POLITICS

Discussions on sex, religion, and politics should be off-limits at work, in bars, and probably a few other places. This is not new advice, but rather a well-known and very often given piece of valuable guidance you can apply in any professional or social situation. These subjects usually inspire heated argument instead of general agreement because people feel deeply about their opinions to the extent that they will often go to great lengths to defend their point of view as the right one, forgetting the concept that we all have a right to our own opinions. It can be tempting to weigh in on these topics, but don't. Be known for your skills, expertise, the kind of person you are, not your opinion on any one of these subjects.

Sex – Of these three taboo topics, this one is the most volatile and can get you into the most actual trouble from job loss to legal/civil actions taken against you by an offended party. In all likelihood you will take a sensitivity course at your workplace, which typically includes harassment, diversity, and bias training. These courses will discuss and provide examples of what not to say and do that could be considered crossing the sensitivity line. Pay attention and take these courses seriously. Your company takes them seriously, and if you blatantly violate any policy related to this topic, you will be putting your career at risk. Sensitivity training is the norm because of past and present abuses, mostly due to people in positions of power abusing people below their level of responsibility. To a large degree, men have been the abusers, but not always.

Religion – Is it okay to discuss religion at work? Maybe, as long as it's not done in an intimidating manner, interferes with employment duties, or creates a situation where you are abusing your authority. It's only natural to foster some familiarity with co-workers, but discussing religion in the workplace falls into a challenging category and is not always a welcome topic. If discussing religion or any other non-work related subject makes your coworkers uncomfortable, you should not discuss it. A conversation that is not a comfortable back-and-forth exchange may feel more like preaching. Religious beliefs are personal and sensitive and not everyone worships the same.[17]

Politics – Discussing politics with someone who does not share your views should also not be done in the workplace. If in your personal life, tempers flare and friendships end over differing political views, why risk discussing politics in the workplace where it is important to have a comfortable working relationship with your coworkers and supervisors?

Liberals and conservatives view our world from different perspectives, and that is good. Balance and different perspectives on political issues are illuminating and frequently helpful. What is not good is that politicians are divisive in the way they attack their colleagues on the other side of the aisle, and yes, both sides do this and have done this from the beginning of time. What is new is that

---

17   https://fairygodboss.com/articles/religion-in-the-workplace

the media now appears to have a political bias that comes across in their presentation of the news. Both the liberal and conservative media have primarily non-biased news programs as well as commentary programs where they tout their political bias.

While I was growing up, there were very few commentary news programs and the local, national, and world news was presented by the three major networks with little or no bias. This presentation was considered the gold standard for both broadcasters and professional journalists. Times have changed and pushing a political perspective rather than reporting with little or no bias is the way of the world now. Why is that? There is a simple answer—because that is where the money is. People watch programming that supports their political views and advertisers allocate their advertising monies according to the demographics of the people watching.

Regarding social media, if like many of us, you have friends and business connections on either side of the political aisle, it is wise to keep your political views off of social media. Posting your political views could cost you a friend or a job. If your friends or business connections post their views, smile at the ones you like and keep quiet on the ones you disagree with.

Many people in corporate America are conservatives while people in education, medicine, non-profits, entertainment, and social programs are often liberals. Of course, these are generalizations—not 100% accurate. But if you are uncomfortable being around people who do not share your political views, look for an environment where your political beliefs are dominant or be prepared to remain silent when and if politics are discussed.

If you are reading this over the holidays, I hope that your family gatherings do not turn into a battle ground, at least for one day. Try to remember that politicians come and go, but your family is your family forever.

DO YOU NEED A MENTOR?

IF YOU ARE READING THIS, I am guessing that you are young, smart, and aggressive. As you prepare to enter the workforce, it's important to understand there is still a lot to learn that the classroom environment cannot teach. It doesn't matter what career path you choose—business, medical, legal, the arts, technical skills, and so on—learning and doing are two very different experiences.

You wouldn't play soccer or any other organized sport without a coach, or take up skiing or golf without lessons, so why take chances with your career?

You're about to engage in a new game that will span forty-plus years. This new game will be on a different playing field, with different rules, and there will be multiple answers or approaches to countless situations. You will need a strategy to leverage your hard-earned education and propel your new career forward so you can get the most out of all that you've invested in yourself so far. So how does a new hire make the right plays in this strange new arena?

Some would say work hard, keep your head down and your nose clean, and you will move up the ranks. Maybe, but why not optimize your chances of success by having a mentor who can share his or her perspective on scenarios you will certainly encounter for the first time?

Examples:

- What if you have an extremely difficult boss or subordinate?

- What if you planned a three-day weekend vacation and the boss asks you to work the weekend to make a deadline?

- How do you handle a new subordinate who has twenty years of experience compared to your six months of experience?

- Why did you not get the promotion, and how do you get promoted next time? What are you doing that you should not, and what are you not doing that you should?

- How do you motivate your team?

- How do you handle ethical issues, like being asked to post an accounting entry that isn't completely accurate—and your boss justifies the entry as "for the good of the team"?

- Strategic issues: If you are an entrepreneur and start your own business or are involved with your family's business, how do you grow the company?

  1. Should you hire from within or through recruiting?
  2. How do you finance the growth?
  3. How much debt is too much?
  4. When putting the annual budget together,

should it be realistic or aggressive, and what are the trade-offs?

- How do you handle unreasonable customers?
- How do you deal with coworkers who don't follow the rules and who create more work and/or unhappy customers?

That is but a small sampling of issues where gaining perspective and direction from a mentor can help you maximize a positive outcome. There are no easy answers, and any answer will require more information and discussion. Having someone you can go to who has lived and breathed these issues far longer than you only makes sense.

As a young man, I did not feel the need for a mentor. I felt that I knew it all or would figure it out. I also felt that my father's experiences had come from the dark ages and were no longer relevant—what a mistake. I didn't know what I didn't know.

My father was the VP of Operations for a manufacturing plant. I became a CPA in public accounting, later in corporate accounting and finance. Although our career paths were very different, there were many overlapping areas, such as working with superiors, peers, subordinates, and the corporate entity. My father would have been a wonderful mentor, as he had been to others, but I wouldn't hear or accept his advice. I was clueless in a world that was unfamiliar to me but certain that I knew it all and could change the world on my own.

By the time I figured out the error of my ways, too much valuable time had passed, and too many mistakes in judgment had been made. In hindsight, my father would have been the best possible mentor for me. He had my best interests at heart and the time and willingness to mentor me. So if this situation sounds familiar, put your pride aside and don't be too headstrong to listen to a parent's advice.

If not your parent, how do you choose the right mentor? Here is one of the best mentoring stories I've ever heard.

Carl Sewell's father owned an automobile dealership in Dallas. Carl looked forward to learning the business and taking it over one day, but he felt the need for a mentor—someone outside of the family. After many months of phone calls and letters, Stanley Marcus—the cofounder of Neiman Marcus—agreed to meet Carl for lunch. After their first lunch, they met for lunch once a month for the next fifteen years. Carl now owns one of the most respected car dealerships in the country, is the author of *Customers for Life*, and is on target to own and operate fifty auto dealerships across the nation.

Carl mentions Stanley Marcus on numerous occasions in his book and in a speech to an executive group, where he tells the story of how Stanley Marcus became his mentor. He said that Mr. Marcus was instrumental to his success in providing excellent customer service and growing his business. Probably the most important takeaway is that quality and value always win.

You may ask why Carl chose and sought out Stanley Marcus in the first place. I believe he sensed there was a link between fine clothing and cars when it came to delivering exceptional customer service. Perhaps he realized that cars—especially luxury cars—were not a commodity, and he wanted to better understand his target market's needs and how to give them exceptional customer service.

Carl struck gold with his mentor, but what did Stanley Marcus get out of the deal, and why did he agree to meet with Carl for fifteen years? Experienced executives in the twilight of their career love to tell stories and welcome an eager audience. They like to give advice, and even more, they like to hear how their advice works out. Having a mentor is a two-way deal, like any other relationship. You have to give to receive. That is, Carl did not provide an endless list of problems for Stanley to solve. Much of the time, he listened to Stanley's stories and worked out how to apply the life lessons to his specific situation.

If you are still in high school or college but have not decided what you want to do for a living, start laying the groundwork for building professional relationships by talking to people already in the workforce about what they do for a living. If you have already graduated and started work, start with relationships already developed and add new relationships. Maybe these conversations will align with your interests as sources of information to help you select your field of study and/or to map out your career-path goals.

You might have family, friends, or friends of classmates who would be good candidates. Go talk to them. Ask them what they do. If they give you a short one-liner, ask them to elaborate. Ask how they decided on their career. Engage them with open-ended questions and let them talk without interruption. If they ask why you want to know, tell them you are trying to figure out what you want to study and what kind of professional career you want. The goal is not to have a mentor at the end of the conversation, but to begin a relationship for future questions and discussions.

After talking to several people, you will be in a position to identify a mentor target who is compatible with you. There are no hard-and-fast rules for mentors, and it doesn't have to be a pairing that lasts for the life of your career. Instead, it may be more appropriate to occasionally make a call to one of your many contacts to discuss an issue you are having at work. After your contact spends that time sharing experiences with you, be sure to follow up and share your progress.

If you find one or two people you believe will be good mentor material, *do not* ask them to be your mentors right away, as this is a major commitment, and you do not want to pop the question until the time is right. Timing is everything, and you will know when the time is right. Continue developing the relationship by periodically contacting them to discuss various issues, always being respectful and always asking if they have time to talk. You need to do most of the listening and be sure not to overstay your welcome. If the time spent with your potential mentor(s) is useful and win-win for all parties, the right time to commit to a mentoring relationship will present itself naturally.

You most likely will not find someone with Stanley Marcus's stature to be your mentor. Carl was able to land Stanley Marcus as a mentor because his family was in the same social circles as Mr. Marcus. Your family's circle of friends may not be in the top social circle, but it is probably larger than you realize, especially if you consider friends of friends. Also, having "achieved high levels of success" is not a must-have for selecting a mentor. Relevant experience is more important, though a high level of success is nice to have. A successful person is not necessarily a good mentor. It only means he or she has mastered a discipline and monetized it.

Your company's code of conduct can serve as a model for the ideal mentor, and having a positive attitude will enhance your self-confidence for approaching potential mentors. These things will put you head and shoulders above the competition.

If you work for a large organization, you may find someone in the organization who could be an exceptional mentor. There are business coaches and life coaches who "mentor" for a fee, though I do not recommend this for people new to the workplace. There should be people in your network who have experienced what you are going through and are—most likely—willing to help you just from a pay-it-forward perspective. I do recommend paid consultants for seasoned executives struggling with a specific issue.

Preferably, there needs to be a link between your career goals and your mentor's experience. Although Carl Sewell was not in the luxury clothing business like Stanley Marcus, they both were in the business of providing the very best customer service for luxury products. Additionally, along the way, Carl Sewell picked up other mentors and/or consultants to help streamline processes necessary to improve both efficiency and customer service.

A mentor should be a been-there-done-that person who has at least one responsibility similar to your responsibilities. There might be a one-for-one relationship, like having the same position, or one or two areas of your responsibilities are the same, like managing shipping operations, and supervision of frontline staff. A one-size-fits-all mentor is generally a leader who is successful in a changing environment. This would include turning a failing business into a profitable business or successfully navigating organizational change such as mergers and acquisitions, reorganizations, or systems changes. This type of mentor has a broad understanding of what makes people successful. Look for that person.

Your mentor will be an important part of your network, and through that person, you have the opportunity to meet other successful people. Leverage the opportunities—successful people hang together.

Then, too, finding a mentor is not necessarily a once-and-done proposition. As you grow in your position and responsibilities, your needs change and grow. Toward that end, you may need new and different mentors as well.

Regardless of whether you graduated from high school, trade school, or college, a mentor can be a huge benefit. And don't forget to pay it forward. Paying it forward will also help hone your ability to find the right mentors over your career life.

Whether or not you find a mentor, always mirror the actions of successful people. Learn from individuals in your organization who have a positive and upward trajectory, as well as from other successful people you meet along the way. Choose your friends carefully and spend time with people who have positive goals and aspirations.

CONSTRUCTIVE CRITICISM

From time to time, you will receive constructive criticism from supervisors, coworkers, friends, and family. For most people, giving constructive criticism is difficult because people realize you don't want to hear it. It is especially difficult if they know you to be someone who puts up walls and can be defensive. If people with your best interests in mind see things that you cannot, but these things could make your life happier, easier, and better, wouldn't you want to hear them? So leave the door open for people to provide constructive criticism.

My dad often said that one should only give advice or constructive criticism in two situations: when it is life and death or if someone asks for advice. I try to live by this mantra, but you will have periodic performance reviews required by your company. You may also receive intermittent constructive criticism around daily activities, like a written document, organization of an electronic spreadsheet, an email you sent, an interaction you had with a coworker, or the like. Some constructive criticism will be superficial and easy to fix, some well-intentioned but off the mark, or a direct and hurtful hit (in this case, it is not constructive—it is just criticism). Keep an open mind and think about what was said or written so that you do not become defensive.

I remember talking to the corporate customer service team at Tuesday Morning, Inc. They fielded calls from customers throughout the country all day, every day. Some of the complaints were serious and required immediate action. But I will never forget being told that every call, no matter how trite, had an element of truth the company needed to address to provide better customer service. Essentially, customers are always right—even when they aren't. The company must continually meet customers' expectations in order to sell to them today as well as tomorrow.

Whether we're talking about customers buying products or services or employees working in exchange for a paycheck, the core concept is the same: there is always a customer, and sometimes the customer is your boss. If your boss tells you that your can-do attitude that you are proud of isn't quite up to par with expectations, you have to figure out how to appease your customer. So when someone criticizes you, dig deep. You may find that the criticism is right on and that you will be a better person, worker, spouse, and so on if you make some changes.

Constructive criticism needs to be taken seriously, as corrective action can change your life for the better. Think about it. Conflict facilitates change, and not all conflict is bad, just like not all changes are bad. Ultimately, the moment of conflict must result in a change, or it will continue to be a source of conflict. Criticism feels like conflict, but if you embrace it as a positive and accept the needed change, you will position yourself to improve and grow professionally and/or personally. You will be happier and more successful in the long run.

I still remember constructive criticism received over forty years ago from my college roommate that has made a difference in my life. I was such a nerd. In fact, I don't remember many of the compliments and praise received over my career, but I definitely remember the hard-to-hear criticism that ultimately shaped my success and still does. It is important to embrace constructive criticism rather than to run from it. I know this advice sounds easy, but it will sometimes be hard.

QUESTION

Here's a question one of my college professors asked our class. In the workplace, will you have more difficulty performing the analysis or obtaining the data necessary to do the analysis? Most got the answer wrong… the answer is obtaining the relevant data.

In school, you are given data in textbooks and challenged with testing on that information, essentially solving problems from provided resources. In the real world, you may be asked to solve problems without being given the necessary data. It is incumbent on you to walk the minefield to get the correct or more appropriately relevant data. Some examples of problems you may face in obtaining the needed and correct data follows.

Example from WWII—During World War II, numerous planes were shot down, and something needed to be done to improve the survival rate. Engineers were called to analyze the problem and recommend a solution. The engineers examined numerous planes at the airstrip and recommended armor plating over the fuselage where the planes had been pierced by enemy fire. The plating was heavy and made the planes sluggish, and even more planes were shot down after the plating was added. What went wrong? The engineers selected the wrong sample of planes to examine. The engineers sampled planes that made it back to the airfield instead of the planes that were shot down. If they had examined the planes that were shot down, they might have recommended additional plating to protect the pilots and the engines. Instead, they reinforced the fuselage, which was not as critical as the pilots and the engines.

You may be asked to evaluate the most recent advertising program to determine whether it is a success or not. Obtaining data from a variety of systems, as well as people, is the challenge.

- Suppose you request data from one of many systems (accounting, operations, warehouse, etc.) and inadvertently pull budgeted data instead of actuals or data from time periods that are not comparable.
- If you rely on others to provide data, it is possible that warehouse or buying department personnel may either accidentally or possibly intentionally give you bad data to make themselves look good.

If this happens, hopefully you or your supervisor will recognize the bad data before the report goes to the higher-ups. If the report goes to the higher-ups with bad data, you will have your first black mark. Get several black marks, and you may soon become a former employee.

A personal example occurred early in my career. I was performing a cost recovery audit at a landlord's mall offices. My coworker and I requested the needed data for our audit two weeks before our cross-country trip. When we arrived, only half of the data requested was provided. The controller stated that his boss, the president of his company, had given him a large project, and he did not have time to collect our requested data. With only a week to do our work before we were to fly home, we called our boss to update him on our situation. He was not sympathetic and told us to "figure it out." Our solution was to contact our company's mall management liaison to see if he could put pressure on the mall's controller. This approach worked, and we obtained the information just in time to complete the audit and catch our flight.

During your career, you will be asked to solve problems. Some of these problems might include:

- Productivity issues
- Accuracy issues
- Various analytical issues
- Human relations issues
- Quality versus speed versus cost issues

It will be your responsibility to obtain the relevant data for analysis in order to form valid conclusions and make appropriate recommendations. You will not necessarily be working in a vacuum, but you may be working with one or two or more people. Not surprisingly, these people may give their opinion of what is causing the "problem," which may conflict with other people's opinions. You may find there is an abundance of finger pointing in corporate America. For example, if a new software package is not performing as expected:

- The software sales team may point fingers at your third-party installer or the users in your company.

- The third-party installer may point fingers at the software sales team saying the software was not designed to do what you expect.

MPG – MANAGE YOUR PROFESSIONAL GROWTH

You are in charge of your happiness.
You are in charge of your career and its growth.
You are in charge of your choices.

Yes, there are things outside of your control, but you are in control of your attitude and the choices you make that impact your happiness and your career. Remember to check your immediate reactions and to swap them out for purposeful actions—act, don't react.

Maybe you didn't get the promotion, and someone you think is less worthy got it. It's natural to feel disappointed or upset at first, but focusing on those personal emotions will not change anything. You won't feel better, and it won't change the fact that someone else got the promotion you felt you deserved. Most importantly, not only will it *not* prepare you to seize the next opportunity but it actually might get in your way. You can't be disappointed or upset and not show it. It will reflect in your body language, your attitude, and it won't look anything like the can-do attitude your superiors are watching for in candidates for promotion.

Rather than waste time and energy reacting to any disappointment that might arise from management decisions, use that energy to do a self-assessment. Not because you did anything wrong, but to identify what you can improve upon and add to your skill sets that will make you a better choice for promotion next time. Act on what you can control rather than reacting to what is not within your control. Your growth, what you do to make yourself competitive, relevant, and invaluable, is always within your control. You may ask yourself, what does Jane provide—attitude, performance, leadership, accuracy, drive, great ideas to improve productivity, etc.—that I do not? Maybe the boss doesn't like you or seems uncomfortable around you, or you don't like the boss or feel uncomfortable around him or her. Is there anything within your control that is causing this unease? Do you stiffen when the boss approaches? Is your body language defensive, or open and receptive? Are you dismissive to the boss's ideas or directions? What about interactions with coworkers? What are your strengths and weaknesses in influencing each person you work with?

STRESS

Don't let superiors, coworkers, or subordinates see you stressed out because they may see this as a sign that you cannot handle your responsibilities. Perception is every bit as important as reality.

GOSSIP

Don't talk behind anyone's back unless the conversation might benefit company operations or profitability. Wherever possible, keep the target person in the loop. Stay out of company politics and gossip.

PICK YOUR BATTLES

Never put yourself in a position where you win the battle but lose the war. Consider the consequences of your actions. You will encounter situations where the cost of winning a battle is too high, or you may not know the cost of winning. You may have a difference of opinion with your boss on overtime, workload, an appraisal, dress code, your boss's management style, and so forth, and you may win the argument, but your boss will probably label you as a difficult employee. He or she may give up on you and start watching for the opportunity to replace you. Every time you raise a difficult and/or controversial issue, you have to ask yourself if the juice is worth the squeeze.

You can only control yourself, not your coworkers and not your boss. There is always something you can change to improve how effective you are, which—in turn—affects how others perceive you. Take purposeful control of the choices you make. Continuously invest in developing your ability to influence the behavior of others and achieving the levels of success and happiness you seek.

Don't seek happiness. Happiness is like an orgasm: if you think about it too much, it goes away. Keep busy and aim to make someone else happy and you might find you get some as a side effect.

—Tim Minchin, comedian, actor, writer (University of Western Australia commencement speech, 2013)

PART III
MOVING UP

MAKE LEARNING A LIFELONG JOURNEY

WHERE YOU WORK IS ALSO where you can learn. Experience as many jobs as possible before graduation. Exposure to various jobs will provide perspective on:

- Industries and jobs you may or may not like
- Various management styles
- Experience in the world of work itself

Though it looks bad after graduation, job hopping while in school is good for you. Experience in various jobs may help you identify something very important to your future job happiness—products or services that interest you.

If you have an internship, this experience could add to your starting salary, and that company may offer you a job upon graduation. An internship with a name-brand company could add significantly to your starting salary and help you develop skills necessary for the working world, broaden your network of contacts, and sharpen your effective communication skills.

Be a lifelong learner in your work and personal life.

Certifications, additional skill sets, and master's degrees, etc. will add value to your value.

Four timeless principles that Allen Questrom—former CEO of Federated Department Stores, Neiman Marcus, Barneys New York, and JCPenney—discussed in his convocation speech[18] at Boston University School of Business follow:

> Dare to be your genuine and trustworthy self. Great leaders and inventors are seldom conformists or imitators. They are original, with the courage to look at what is and to dare to envision a better way by thinking outside the square.
>
> Remember, even if you are the boss, it isn't all about you. The greatest leaders are passionate and purpose and action driven, but they don't succeed by themselves. Leaders provide the strategy, but its successful execution requires investors, employees, and customers buying into the strategy. While managers aspire to top leadership jobs, they need to inspire a lot of people to reach that goal. A successful manager must carefully control scarce resources of time, money, and people, and that is not necessarily dependent on how smart you are. You will make mistakes along the way because no one is perfect. This is part of the learning process, and it's what you do with your mistakes that will matter most in the long run. Admit that you don't have all the answers. The best leaders surround

---

18 https://youtu.be/-u09kcffcpQ.

themselves with the best people, so they have the right people to go to when they don't know the answers. No one gets to where they are on their own. The sooner you recognize this, the more effectively you'll demonstrate leadership qualities.

Any business is a people business. Managers can get bogged down in managing and miss opportunities in plain sight, like empowering employees and customers by seeking them out, walking around with them, asking them a lot of questions about the business or the product, really listening to the answers, being present… and observing their concerns and reactions. This not only gives the manager a lot of essential information, but also draws everyone into the team effort, making it their game.

Get your head out of your apps. Make time for a personal life that includes a significant other. As much as technology can do for us, it cannot make us lovable, so put down the phone and treat romance as if it were a start-up. Once you have romanced and caught the partner of your dreams, don't assume that the deal is done. Keep the romance alive and you will be rewarded. Humanize and personalize yourself. Believe in yourself. Lose the fear and find the courage to take risks. And finally, be mindfully present. Get your head out of your apps and notice the color of someone's eyes.

We know that today, education is still the key to real and lasting freedom—it is still true today. So it is now up to us to cultivate that hunger for education in our own lives and in those around us. And we know that hunger is still out there—we know it.

—Michelle Obama (Dillard University commencement speech, 2014)

We grow and learn by doing difficult/unfamiliar things. You might remember how difficult it was to jump into a swimming pool the first time when you were a youngster, but after doing this a couple of times; you found it to be fun. Parents often push their children through situations so they learn that pushing through uncomfortable things will allow them to grow, and they will one day be able to push through on their own. As you enter the workforce, you will be doing some things that are difficult, and you will need to push through.

You have learned a lot in your many years of education, but you need experience, time-in-position, and the right title before making bold changes and strategic decisions. We are all eager to put our knowledge to work and show the world that we are ready to contribute. But we need to slow down, take a breath, and learn our new roles in the workplace before we begin telling our bosses and coworkers what needs to be changed.

Years ago, I was recruiting on a college campus for an entry-level position for a Fortune 500 company. The person being interviewed told me that his college education prepared him to make strategic corporate decisions that are generally the responsibility of the C-suite executives (chief executive officer, chief financial, chief marketing officer, etc.) or maybe the EVPs (executive vice presidents). I repeatedly told this candidate that he was getting ahead of himself and that he was being interviewed for an entry-level position. I truly hope that he learned something from the interview and changed his approach for future interviews.

For those who get an offer and start work in a small, medium, or large organization, it is important to learn the business by listening, observing, and asking. Don't try to be an expert around the experts. Your new organization has a specific job for you to perform and probably a specific methodology for doing so. You can't make solid recommendations for change until you have some experience in doing things their way and have established yourself as an expert in your role as well as someone with values that align with the company's mission statement.

In a meeting with two leather tanning experts, the millennial who had never set foot in a tanning factory before tried to tell two men with over forty years in the tanning business how their operations should run. If you do this, you will be thought of as a know-it-all, and the people you are trying to impress will lose respect for you.

Maybe the process you are learning needs to change. Maybe "they" have always done it that way and "they" do not know why or how their work fits into the big picture. The time may come when you are asked to evaluate the process and make recommendations, but until that time, keep learning. When you are certain you have an idea that will improve the process and not disrupt anything else, that is the time to suggest change. Respect the hard work of those working at a company and build your reputation to include a mutual respect so that you can actually make changes with little or no resistance.

So take your time, keep learning, and be patient!

> Benjamin Jefferson said, *To be proud of knowledge is to be blind with light.* In other words—the more knowledge you gain, the more you realize how little knowledge you really have.

> *Live as if you were to die tomorrow.*
> *Learn as if you were to live forever.*
>
> —Mahatma Gandhi

"HOW TO WIN FRIENDS AND INFLUENCE PEOPLE"

In 1936, Dale Carnegie published *How to Win Friends and Influence People*, which has become one of the most successful books in American history.[19] He wrote it during a time when people were moving off the farms to live in cities. People going to work in factories meant working relationships with coworkers and clients became increasingly important. Even though the book was written many years ago, it continues to set sales records each year, serving as a cornerstone for the Dale Carnegie Company, which focuses on professional training and development solutions. So much of his rock-solid advice is still relevant to this day.

Some the key takeaways from Dale's book follow:

BE GENUINELY INTERESTED IN OTHER PEOPLE AND WHAT THEY HAVE TO SAY.

Why? Because people are most interested in themselves. Express an interest in everyone you meet or come in contact with, not just the people who can promote you,

---

19 Dale Carnegie, How to Win Friends and Influence People (Simon & Schuster, 1936).

give you a raise, or help you socially. Showing interest in everyone will ultimately benefit you—try it, and you will see. You may benefit by receiving a warm feeling or by the increased respect of a subordinate or peer. Greet people with animation and enthusiasm. When your phone rings, say hello in tones that indicate how pleased you are to have the person call.

Another twist on the above comes from Tim Minchin:

Respect people with less power than you. I don't care if you're the most powerful cat in the room; I will judge you on how you treat the least powerful... So there!

—Tim Minchin, comedian, actor, writer (University of Western Australia commencement speech, 2013)

SMILE OFTEN, ESPECIALLY WHEN GREETING PEOPLE, AND MAKE SURE YOUR SMILE IS GENUINE.

Don't fake it. Mean it! Sometimes you don't feel like smiling, so then what? Force yourself to smile, and that will tend to make you feel happier too. You have to stand up straight and say it with feeling. Everybody in the world is seeking happiness, and there is one sure way to find it. That is by controlling your thoughts. Happiness doesn't depend on outward conditions—it depends on inner conditions.

When asked in passing how he was, a well-known CFO in Dallas always answered, "Wonderful." You can't say wonderful with your head down and shoulders slumped.

REMEMBER THAT A PERSON'S NAME IS, TO HIM OR HER, THE SWEETEST AND MOST IMPORTANT SOUND.

If you are introduced and forget the person's name, ask that the name be repeated. It is better to ask for the name again than to pretend you know it and not use it.

BE A GOOD LISTENER.

Encourage others to talk about themselves and their interests. Don't interrupt. Use the pronoun "I" less.

TALK IN TERMS OF THE OTHER PERSON'S INTEREST.

When meeting with a client, your priority is to develop a relationship. If the client wants to talk about sailing, his favorite sports team, Sunday's golf game, the grandkids, or whatever, let him. Don't interrupt. And you will find that when you do talk about business, you will have ample time to do so, and more likely, a reciprocation of attention.

MAKE THE OTHER PERSON FEEL IMPORTANT AND DO IT SINCERELY.

In other words, "Do unto others as you would have others do unto you." Everybody wants the approval of those they come in contact with, the recognition of their true worth, and to feel that they are important in their little world. Nobody wants to listen to cheap, insincere flattery instead of sincere appreciation.

IF YOU ARE WRONG, ADMIT IT.

If you are wrong and defend your position, your opposition will come on much stronger to prove you wrong. If, on the other hand, you admit to being wrong quickly, openly, and with enthusiasm, your opposition may take a magnanimous attitude of minimizing your mistake to build their self-esteem and feelings of self-importance.

As an example, if you are stopped for speeding and admit that you were wrong, the police officer may surprise you with a warning instead of a ticket. The benefits of admitting you were wrong apply in the workplace as well as in your personal life.

If you have an angry customer, your willingness to take the blame for quality or other issues may take all of the fight out of your customer.

If we know that we are going to catch hell anyhow, isn't it better to beat the other guy to it and do it ourselves? Isn't it much easier to listen to self-criticism than to bear condemnation from alien lips?

IF YOUR TEMPER IS AROUSED, AND THE OTHER GUY'S TEMPER FOLLOWS, IT BECOMES DIFFICULT TO AGREE.

At times like these, both parties should put their "guns" down and lower the volume in order to calmly and rationally discuss differences. Will you be the leader in this situation to call for everybody to put their "guns" down?

In Carnegie's chapter, "A Simple Way to Make a Good First Impression," he shares an advertisement that was published at Christmas by a department store in New York City:

> **"The Value of a Smile at Christmas"**
> It costs nothing but creates much.
>
> It enriches those who receive, without
> impoverishing those who give.

CLASSROOM TO CAREER

It happens in a flash and the memory
of it sometimes lasts forever.

None are so rich that they can get along without it,
and none so poor but are richer for its benefits.

It creates happiness in the home, fosters goodwill
in a business and is the countersign of friends.

It is rest to the weary, daylight to the discouraged,
sunshine to the sad, and Nature's best antidote for trouble.

Yes, it cannot be bought, begged, borrowed,
or stolen, for it is something that is no earthly
good to anybody till it is given away!

And if, in the last-minute rush of Christmas buying,
some of our salespeople should be too tired to give
you a smile, may we ask that you leave one of yours?

For nobody needs a smile so much as
those who have none left to give!

Whoever is happy will make others happy.

—Anne Frank

ATTITUDE, PERSONALITY, AND CAPACITY TO LEARN

PHIL HILL SPENT THIRTY-SIX YEARS in information technology (IT), mostly in an executive position with Zale Corporation, Lomas Mortgage, Prudential Mortgage, and BNSF Railway. Phil has enjoyed mentoring small groups to large groups of eighty-five. Many of Phil's mentoring materials are sourced from Stephen R. Covey's book, *The 7 Habits of Highly Effective People*. A natural leader and motivator who brings out the best in his team, Phil offers the following thoughts.

Attitude, personality, and capacity to learn are things everyone is expected to bring with them to a job. These areas of development are not the responsibility of companies to provide as part of on-the-job training. They will either be assets and skills or baggage that drags one down and are solely the individual's responsibility.

If you have not yet developed a positive attitude, good personality, and capacity to learn, what then? You can still develop these attributes for your next job or the job after that. Life experience and work experience will teach you if you are open-minded, willing to learn, and purposely expose yourself to situations where these attributes are required and consequences for poor performance are implemented.

Some insights:

- "Not my job" speaks to attitude and capacity to learn. People who aspire to be average only do "their share of the work." If you want to be average, just do your share. People who strive to excel will always do more than their share and produce more than their peers.

- Dependability is one of the most sought-after traits in any employee. People who can't be available when they are needed—or won't show up for the job—bring little or no value to a company regardless of their abilities, and so they are destined to be replaced.

- Leave drama at home. Where possible, work out differences with your coworkers without involving your boss.

- Be supportive of your boss. Bosses can and will be demanding, with high standards. Attitude regarding workload does not play well. Bosses have staffing constraints and production and quality needs. But if you are unable to complete your assigned work on time, or if you feel that you are working an inordinate amount of time to complete your tasks, it may be time to take action. If the person who performed the tasks before you is still around, he or she might help review your work and suggest shortcuts, but if not, schedule time with your supervisor. Before scheduling a meeting with your boss, prepare a list of your weekly or monthly tasks with an approximate time spent on each task. It might be helpful to indicate if the time spent has increased or decreased and why. Your supervisor may suggest a more efficient approach, identify aspects of your tasks that are no longer necessary, suggest that your efficiency should improve over time, offload tasks to another team member, or indicate that there is nothing s/he can do to reduce your workload for the short term or even long term. In the end, you may or may not like the answer, but you will have an answer.

- Be a team player and a problem solver.

- Be open to discussion, but don't be argumentative. Once a decision is made, give it 100 percent of your support.

- Anticipate questions rather than being awkward or uninspired. This attribute will help prepare you for promotion.

- Adopt an attitude of persistence to get the job done. Given the choice, employers often prefer persistence over smarts.

- Come in early, stay late, and offer to help with projects.

- Be confident in your skills and abilities, but always have a willingness to learn.

When you change jobs, and you will, be forewarned that potential employers will call previous employers to ask about your work history. Attitude, personality, and capacity to learn will most likely be included in the questions as well as dependability. Even a part-time job or entry-level job can affect future job prospects.

Nothing can stop the man with the right mental attitude from achieving his goal; nothing on earth can help the man with the wrong mental attitude.

—Thomas Jefferson

TRADE UP TO BIGGER PROBLEMS

OPPORTUNITIES ARE SOMETIMES DISGUISED AS problems in all areas of our lives. All work environments have problems hiding in plain sight. As you might guess, the bigger the job responsibilities, the bigger the problems. So, if you want to move up in your organization, trade your smaller problems for bigger ones. Some examples:

- Volunteer for a tough assignment and work endlessly to solve the problem.

- If your boss comes to you with new responsibilities, be ready and appreciative of your boss's faith in your ability and potential. Don't say it is not your job or raise concerns about your ability to learn and perform the new duties.

- If your company has a reduction in staff, volunteer for one or two of the key responsibilities of the departed employee. Your attitude and initiative in seeking out larger problems may help ensure you are not part of the reduction in force.

- Volunteer to train a new employee, perform an out-of-the-ordinary analysis, help open a new company location, or assist with physical inventories. The more you learn and contribute, the more value you bring to the table.

- If you are a leader, volunteer to head up a task force or assemble a team to solve a problem. If you are not a leader, volunteer to be on that team in a support role.

Another way to frame the bigger problem philosophy is to act like an owner of the company. A friend of mine worked for a small company with a disorganized warehouse. She saw the disarray in the warehouse, and because she took pride in her place of work, she took the time to reorganize the clutter. After a short time, she was promoted to warehouse manager and later to successive management positions. She eventually moved on to own her own successful company.

There are smaller things you can do to act like an owner of the company and set an example for others while demonstrating leadership. How many people walking through the office will step over trash in the aisles? It takes a special person to stop and pick it up, and people will notice. You will be noticed if you make coffee when the pot is empty. They will especially take notice if you regularly leave the kitchen cleaner than you found it. In general, if you see something that needs doing, do it! These small things get you noticed so that you stand above the crowd.

Always keep your eyes and ears open for additional responsibilities, and let it be known that you have successfully taken on additional responsibilities in the past. Having a history of taking on bigger problems will put you on the fast track for promotion.

Would this approach benefit you in other areas of your life? I think so. Look for opportunities to try it out. You may be pleasantly surprised by the reactions you receive.

TWO HEADS ARE BETTER THAN ONE

TWO DEGREES OF SEPARATION; ANY two strangers are—on average—distanced by precisely 6.6 degrees of separation. You are one degree away from everyone you know, two degrees away from everyone they know, and so on, so that a chain of "a friend of a friend" statements can be made to connect any two people in a maximum of 6.6 steps.

You will not have all the answers, but someone within two degrees of separation will probably be able to help. If you do not have the answers, ask for help. You are more than likely to have a better outcome in the long run. While being a problem solver is important, sometimes you will need to ask questions rather than muddle through and do something wrong.

Many professional organizations support open forums on the internet where you can post messages and ask for help on a variety of issues. In addition, you could pose questions either to an individual or team of people at your company or to an individual in your professional network. I have a colleague who constantly networks. He is continuously looking for the best practices. He regularly asks his competitors what systems—as well as what processes—they use to manage their businesses.

Don't be afraid to ask for help.

WHEN SOMETHING GOES WRONG

Things go wrong; it is part of life. With proper planning, policies, and procedures, things that go wrong can be minimized. But when thing go wrong, it is important to handle properly. Some concepts that are important to remember when these situations occur include integrity, open-mindedness, taking responsibility, and asking for help. Addressing things that go wrong almost always provides a learning opportunity. Examples of areas where things go wrong:

- Angry customers
- Spreadsheet errors, data errors, spelling errors
- Personnel issues
- Missed deadlines
- Budget variances
- Missed quotas

When something goes wrong:

- Take responsibility rather than placing blame.
- Develop a plan of action/process to ensure that the problem does not happen again.

When something goes wrong, you will also need to decide if it is necessary to inform your boss. This answer will depend on a variety of things, such as your boss' need to know, your relationship with your boss, the seriousness of the problem, whether the issue affects other departments as well as intercompany relationships. When discussing with your boss, your boss may want to know:

- That it won't happen again and what you are doing to ensure that it does not happen again

OR

- What caused the problem and what you are doing to fix it so that it does not happen again

Know who you are dealing with and respond appropriately.

There are generally two types of people. There are those who only want to know what you are doing to fix the problem. These people view explanations of what went wrong as a string of excuses or incompetence. So do *not* provide a detailed history to these people. They do not have the interest or the time to listen and may become agitated and even angry at your long-winded explanation.

Other people are more of the hands-on type and want to know all of the steps that caused the problem.

But if your problem cannot be fixed without budget adjustment, additions to staff, major systems changes, or other changes that are not likely to occur, *be careful*. You may be in a no-win situation where management may not be supportive of your efforts to correct the problem(s).

I can think of many situations where underlings were in

no-win situations. One that comes to mind occurred when senior management went on a merchandise-buying spree without discussing warehouse storage needs with warehouse personnel. Merchandise quickly exceeded warehouse capacity. Every available storage location was in use, and excess merchandise was stored in the aisles. The result was gridlock, and warehouse production came to a screeching halt. The problem, as well as an interim solution, was obvious, but senior management would not get involved and tied the hands of warehouse management—truly a no-win situation.

At one point in my career, I was in a no-win situation, and my boss said, "I know it is not your fault, but you are going to take the blame." This situation reminded me of a joke.

> An outgoing CEO tells the new CEO that he has left three envelopes in his top desk drawer to be used if and when a crisis arises. When the first crisis occurred, the new CEO opened the first envelope. The note inside said to blame the marketing department for an ineffective and expensive marketing campaign. The new CEO survived the crisis. When the second crisis occurred, the new CEO opened the second envelope, which said to blame distribution for delays and errors in shipping. The new CEO survived the second crisis and was feeling pretty good when the third crisis emerged. When he opened the third and final envelope, the note said *prepare three envelopes.*

The point is, if you are in a no-win situation, and you do not have enough political strength to counteract a senior person placing blame on you, you may need to look for another job. The environment in your present company does not bode well for your long-term employment. You may not know if blame for a no-win situation is coming your way after the first or third envelope. Your chances of survival are much greater if your senior manager is on the third envelope.

DON'T BE AN ENABLER

ARE YOU WILLING TO PITCH in and help when there is a need? If yes, you are the kind of employee every manager and company needs. But here is where it gets slippery. Suppose one of your coworkers is having problems at home with a spouse, child, parent, medical, substance, or even a financial issue. Because of these issues, this coworker asks you, without telling your boss, to help him with his work. Being a good person, you gladly pitch in and help. You work extra hours and get the job(s) done. The problem comes when this arrangement never ends, and you are working long hours at a feverish pace to do both your job and your coworker's.

How does this situation appear to your boss? Your coworker may seem to get his job done quickly and accurately while you, on the other hand, are working long hours and appear stressed. If this were the only criteria used to measure who gets a promotion, it probably won't be you.

So how do you get out of this unpleasant situation? If you confide in the boss, you will damage the confidential agreement you have with your coworker. The best solution is to talk with your coworker. Find a quiet place where you will not be interrupted. Tell your coworker that you have been doing part of his job with the understanding that this situation would be temporary. Since this arrangement has continued long past the temporary stage, it is time to establish a short timeline to transition the work back to the coworker. If the transition takes place, all is well. If not, you will need to discuss this with your supervisor.

IMPOSTOR SYNDROME

PER WIKIPEDIA, IMPOSTOR SYNDROME (ALSO known as impostor phenomenon, impostorism, fraud syndrome, or the impostor experience) is a psychological pattern in which an individual doubts his or her skills, talents, or accomplishments and has a persistent internalized fear of being exposed as a "fraud." Despite external evidence of their competence, those experiencing this phenomenon remain convinced they are frauds and do not deserve all they have achieved. Early research focused on the prevalence among high-achieving women though impostor syndrome has since been recognized to affect both men and women equally.

It has been estimated that nearly 70 percent of individuals will experience signs and symptoms of impostor syndrome at least once in their life. Often, the syndrome arises due to a new professional setting. If you are pushing yourself—or maybe a supervisor is pushing you—to advance and achieve, you will be in new and unfamiliar situations, both of which are important for personal growth.

It is important to fight impostor syndrome, because it can stifle potential by preventing people from pursuing growth opportunities. Focus on your strengths and qualifications, not on what you have not done.

Are you a perfectionist? Impostor syndrome can be related to perfectionism, where you may feel pressure to perform at your absolute best 100 percent of the time. Maybe the following or something like this has happened to you. Are you uncomfortable with promotions or additional responsibilities because you do not feel ready or because you are being promoted or given additional responsibility faster than your peers? If so, you may have impostor syndrome. It is normal to feel nervous in these situations. And nobody is going to be perfect on day one. Speak to your supervisor about your concerns. Maybe he or she had some of the same feelings as he or she moved up the ranks and has some thoughts to help and guide you in your new role. A loved one or mentor may also provide some helpful insight.

Another thing to consider is that your supervisor probably sees something in you that sets you apart from your peers. There is a reason that you got the promotion. Your supervisor feels that you are the right person for the job and will succeed.

> *The trouble with the world is that the stupid are cocksure and the intelligent are all full of doubt.*
>
> —Bertrand Russell

> *I still believe that at any time the no-talent police will come and arrest me.*
>
> —Mike Myers, actor, comedian

When you feel like an impostor, try to remember you are not alone. It's normal to strive for perfection, though it's impossible to achieve it, and everyone stresses to some degree with feelings of insecurity. Shift your focus to your accomplishments, to recognizing what others in the workplace see in you, and let that be affirmation that you are just fine.

TAKING A LEADERSHIP ROLE

Management is about persuading people to do things they do not want to do, while leadership is about inspiring people to do things they never thought they could.

—Steve Jobs[20]

No matter the role you have now, if your goal is working toward a management position or even being recognized as a leader among your peers and having more responsibilities, it will be important to demonstrate the appropriate leadership qualities in everything you do at all times. The people in your company who can give you the opportunities you are seeking will know what to look for, so desirable leadership qualities—or the lack of—will be apparent even before you have leadership responsibilities.

Leadership has nothing to do with seniority, titles, or position in the hierarchy of a company. It isn't something only provided by members of management, and it isn't something all members of management excel in just because they are in management. You can have positive and negative leaders—and those who aren't leaders at all—in

---

20 "Steve Jobs. AZQuotes.com, Wind and Fly LTD," 2020, https://www.azquotes.com/quote/1059342.

any scenario in life because leadership is simply the ability to influence others. People with the ability to influence either create a path of positivity or negativity that others around them follow instead of forging their own way.[21]

An employee who exhibits negative leadership qualities might, for example, have a tendency to complain in a confident manner and in a strategic way that causes others to see the same negative views. A very important positive leadership quality is being able to influence others to embrace a big change and make the best of it. Which employee would any company prefer to work with and/or promote?

There are countless resources available on the internet about leadership qualities and how to develop and recognize each of them, and these lists vary from one to the next. Below are a few common core qualities that are on most of the lists, and they are the most desirable and best place to start.

RESPECT

Leadership status is granted, but influence and respect are earned. Setting a good example consistently will inspire positive outcomes and directly affect whether you earn respect and are able to influence others. To improve your levels of influence and respect:

- Set a good example. (See the "Dos and Don'ts" chapter.)

---

21 Travis Bradberry, "What Makes a Leader? The Essence of Great Leadership Lies in the Right Definition," https://www.inc.com/amrita-khalid/tech-trends-forecast-future-amy-webb.html.

- Connect with people empathetically and make them feel important. (See the excerpts from Dale Carnegie's book, *How to Win Friends and Influence People*.)
- Build a network of long-lasting relationships. (See the chapter "Navigating Corporate America II.")

EFFECTIVE COMMUNICATION

Great leaders know when to talk and when to listen, and they are able to clearly explain their vision and many of the specifics to get the job done. Active listening—including eye contact and expressions of sincere interest—ensures the team feels heard. If you do not listen to your team, they will not follow you.

CONFIDENCE

References to confidence are scattered throughout this book. If you lack confidence in a leadership role, people will spot that quickly. The more you believe in yourself, the more you'll be able to manage stressful situations. People will instinctively recognize that and will follow the appearance of confidence. This trait is exhibited more in nonverbal clues—body language—than through words. Standing tall and not slouching, making eye contact, and not fidgeting will be the first things people notice.

HONESTY also, see the "Integrity" chapter

Contrary to the popular belief that many successful business leaders are inherently dishonest, great leaders treat others as they want to be treated because it's the only real way to make strong connections with others. Dishonest, fake, or insincere habits or practices will quickly derail any career path. Integrity should be a foundational concept for any role, but is definitely a huge factor in success as a leader. As a leader, you may find yourself in tough situations and be tempted to violate your honesty or integrity standards. Don't do it! By taking the high road, your inner self will be at peace versus turmoil. Additionally, your subordinates, superiors, and peers will raise their opinion of your character to the next level. Each time that you do what is hard, but right, it gets easier to do as future difficult situations arise.

VISION

Jack Welch, former chairman and CEO of General Electric, said, "Good business leaders create a vision, articulate the vision, passionately own the vision, and relentlessly drive it to completion."[22]

Wouldn't it have been nice to know Steve Job's vision in early 2000? Or how about Jeff Bezos's vision for Amazon, or Larry Page's vision for Google?

All great leaders need a vision they can articulate and drive to completion. Even though you may not be the CEO, you need a vision for yourself and your team. Maybe your vision is to dramatically improve productivity with a new approach or new systems, for example. It takes demonstrating this trait consistently, from the bottom up, to earn the right to make larger changes.

Successful leaders also have a growth mindset. They

---

22 William White, "10 Jack Welch Quotes to Remember from the Former GE CEO," March 2, 2020, https://investorplace.com/2020/03/jack-welch-quotes-to-remember-from-the-former-ge-ceo/.

embrace change and take responsibility for their mistakes while making every effort to learn from them. They are decisive, driven, and focused. You will find a plethora of great resources on the internet that break down lists of leadership qualities and define them, many with workshopping tools to help you develop your own. No matter if you intend to pursue management roles in your career path, or if you want to punch a time clock—with the goal of earning as much as you can each year on a stable schedule with minimal responsibilities—positive leadership qualities will be the key to your success.

Great leaders are almost always great simplifiers, who can cut through argument, debate and doubt, to offer a solution everybody can understand.

—Colin Powell, retired US Army four-star general

Don't just get involved. Fight for your seat at the table. Better yet, fight for a seat at the head of the table.

—President Barack Obama (Barnard College commencement speech, 2012)

Getting Ahead—To get ahead, you must be at the top of the scale in the performance of your job duties. Other key characteristics, traits, support systems, and work history that work in your favor follow as bullet points from various chapters in this book.

- Obtain a go-to person for advice on work-related issues—a mentor.

- Align your personality traits and talents to your career.
- Have a positive attitude and smile.
- Don't just point to problems, solve them or propose recommendations—be a solution maker, not a complainer.
- Trade up to bigger problems.
- Do the right thing and don't say the wrong thing.
- Don't burn bridges.
- Adopt Dale Carnegie's guidelines from *How to Win Friends and Influence People*.
- Be a hard worker—lead by example.
- Have a history of getting the job done by working hard, smart, and creatively.

WHAT ELSE IS NEEDED?

- Visibility—You need to be in front of decision makers on an ongoing basis, otherwise you will be forgotten. This means attending meetings and participating with something positive and meaningful to add to the meeting's topic. It is also important to go to lunch with the team and attend extracurricular activities. If you are an extrovert, participating is easy. However, if you are an introvert, it is probably more difficult.

Extroverts are usually primed and ready to speak on any subject being discussed. Introverts, on the other hand, generally need time to process the topic and their thoughts before speaking. When introverts do speak, their comments are typically insightful, thought provoking, and useful. Their problem is that they are often unable to get airtime to make their case before that moment passes.

Since the majority of workplace culture is extroverted, this issue may be foreign to the boss or meeting leader. One approach to help ensure airtime at meetings would be to have a private conversation with your boss to explain your plight as an introvert. This conversation should go well since it is most likely that your boss wants participation and also wants the best ideas presented. It may sound corny, but consider an agreed-upon signal you can make when you have something to contribute (e.g., a tug on your ear). When this happens, the boss may say, "What do you think?"

Another helpful method to improve your ability to speak in front of groups for both introverts and extroverts would be to join and attend Toastmasters clubs. https://www.toastmasters.org

If you score well on the above criteria, you *will* be considered for the next promotional opportunity.

Something else to consider: Many top universities use the case study method of teaching. I am told that this method is used to foster, encourage, and demand group participation, and here is the reason. All organizations have top-level problems, and often the approach to solve these problems is to call a meeting of all department heads to discuss, research, and decide on a solution. This process frequently pits department heads against each other, and the solution that is usually adopted is presented by the department head that presents the strongest and most convincing solution.

As a cautionary note, this solution may not be the best one presented, but it is adopted due to the department head's presentation skills. This high-wire act may propel the department head forward in the organization, especially if the solution is successful. If unsuccessful, the department head may be forced to take his presentation and persuasion skills to another organization. The point is that visibility can be very important to advancement, but also includes some degree of risk. While this example takes place at the highest levels of the organization, similar situations occur at all levels.

COWORKERS NO MORE

THROUGHOUT THIS BOOK, THERE HAVE been references to promotions, but no discussion on how to handle the new responsibility. Promotions can be difficult, especially when you are responsible for a team of people who were your peers. You are responsible for everyone on your team as well as their related work. You are shifting from 100 percent doer to a leader who does less doing and more leading in order to complete a task.

You must motivate your people and maintain an environment of accountability. Having a participative management style is critical to having people feel empowered and having them feel they make a difference so that results are achieved—good for you and them!

If you feel uncomfortable in this new role, that is natural. New roles and relationships can be uncomfortable for both you and your team, but probably more so for you. On a go-forward basis, you are the boss, responsible for the group's performance: quality, speed, accuracy, customer service, and maybe even the departmental budgets. You are also responsible for appraisals and corrective action discussions as well as hiring and firing responsibilities.

You may wonder how to move from being a peer to being a manager so that you successfully lead your team.

One of the most important things to do from the start is to set the proper tone. Your relationship between you and your team has changed.

How and what do you communicate to your team? A team meeting and/or face-to-face meeting with each member might be appropriate. Points to discuss in your meetings might include:

- Recognizing that this is a new relationship for both you and the team.

- Emphasizing that they are still working with you as much as for you and that you are committed to the team's success.

- Emphasizing that you know each member of the team and that you understand the challenges and difficulties that they face, and, where possible, you will work to find solutions. This first-hand knowledge that you have will work to their advantage versus an outsider assuming the role.

- As the new boss, it should go without saying that, in this new relationship, you will require respect from each of your team members and in turn will respect each of them.

- You might point out that you are open to their suggestions that would improve the team's performance and reduce their pain points.

- If appropriate, point out that, in addition to a change in your role, boundaries may also change. If you have additional responsibilities, which you may or may not fully understand, you may allude to this and discuss at a later date.

As a new manager, you will make mistakes—learn from them.

NAVIGATING CORPORATE AMERICA I

Jeff St. Pierre is young, aggressive, and successful. Before college, Jeff worked for a hazardous materials handling company. After college, he moved to several high-level jobs where he worked for young executives with large egos, which resulted in a fast-paced and high-pressure environment full of learning opportunities. Jeff leveraged his experience with the hazardous materials handling company to found TTN Fleet Solutions. Jeff has tremendous confidence, is extremely perceptive, and offers the following thoughts.

Do not argue with angry people, whether customers, bosses, or coworkers. Be empathetic without accepting responsibility, and let the angry person get it out of his or her system without interruption. Get on the same base as the angry person and allow the individual to be angry.

ANGRY CUSTOMER TECHNIQUES

First rule: Let the customer finish venting without interruption. When there is a pause, interject by saying, "I understand your disappointment in the product. I would be upset if I were in your place."

Then, maybe, "I would like to discuss your situation with my boss, as you may not be the only person experiencing this problem." Ask the customer what he or she wants you/your company to do.

If you do not have the authority to satisfy the person's wish, you might say, "If you like, I will check with my supervisor to see if we can satisfy your request. Would that be okay? Please give me your contact information, and I will let you know what my boss/supervisor thinks about your request."

In many cases, you already know the answer, but this approach gives the customer time to cool off and heads off the possibility of making the situation worse.

If a customer is unhappy with the quality/specifications of the product, don't argue unless you don't mind losing the customer. It could be that the customer requires a higher grade of product. If you satisfy the customer with a better grade per his or her specific requirements, you may retain the customer. This is very important since the cost of retaining a customer is far less expensive than acquiring a new customer.

ANGRY BOSS TECHNIQUES

Your boss might be angry because your staff has not met their sales goals, has exceeded their expense budgets, are late on their project deliverables, etc. You might reply, "I saw the same thing but have not acted yet. I am watching the situation to gather more information before acting. I need to understand the root cause of the issue before making changes."

DIFFICULT BOSSES AND HOSTILE WORK ENVIRONMENTS

Below are two personal experiences with challenging bosses.

- I had one boss who was a yeller and a screamer. He could handle the big stuff, but small stuff drove him crazy. When I was new with the company, he called me into his office, yelled at me for a minor infraction, turned red in the face, and got within inches of my face as he yelled at me. When he finished, I tried to explain, but he started yelling anew, which happened twice until I realized that I needed to let my boss finish his venting. When he finished, I left his office with my tail between my legs, and one by one my officemates came up to me and said, "Congratulations, you're one of us now." Just like the angry customer, it is important to let your boss finish venting without interruption.

- Another boss had a Jekyll-and-Hyde personality. He had major mood swings, and his staff never knew if he was currently Mr. Nice or Mr. Mean.

If you have one of these bosses, you have to ask yourself:

- Can I outlast this boss? Will he or she move up or out in the foreseeable future?

- Am I learning enough in this environment to offset the treatment I am receiving?

At some point in your career, you will have a terrific boss or several really good bosses. Your experiences with the opposite type of boss will help you appreciate a good boss. When you first recognize that you have someone who is good to work for, it might be helpful if you prepare a list of all past and present bosses and put this list where you can find it quickly. Circle or highlight all of the good supervisors you have had. If your tally of bad bosses outweighs the number of good bosses, you will definitely appreciate your good boss. This list becomes particularly beneficial when you have a difficult confrontational moment with your good boss. When this happens, pull out your list and reaffirm your appreciation for your good boss, take a couple of deep breaths, settle down, and get back to work.

HOSTILE WORK ENVIRONMENT

Most of us have heard the term *hostile work environment* and hope we are never subjected to this environment. However, if we are, can we file a successful legal claim for personal damages? While harsh criticism and confrontational conversations are unpleasant, as noted in the above two examples, it does not usually meet the legal standards to satisfy a successful legal claim. To meet that standard, the hostile environment must be so extreme, alarming, daunting, menacing, disturbing, and deliberate as to adversely affect the victim's psyche. This is an extremely high, almost unattainable threshold to pass. "One court has framed the threshold as so outrageous in character and so extreme in degree as to go beyond all possible bounds of decency and to be regarded as atrocious."[23]

Although the odds of a successful legal claim are low, it is a good idea to keep notes on hostile situations including conversations, persons present, dates, and times. These

---

23 Lindsey Novak, "Hostile Work Environment: Intentional Infliction," Creators, March 18, 2021, www.creators.com/read/at-work-lindsey-novak/03/21/hostile-work-environment-intentional-infliction.

notes could be helpful if and when human resources or a senior management person asks for information related to your experience. However, in all likelihood, your best options are, as mentioned above, to ask yourself:

- Can I outlast this boss/individual?
- Am I learning enough in this hostile environment to offset the abuse?

If not, it is time to find another job as soon as possible.

DON'T DRESS LIKE YOUR PEERS UNLESS YOU WANT TO *BE* LIKE YOUR PEERS.

Dress to excel and to climb the corporate ladder. Wear clothes that fit into your office environment, but trend toward the next level up. While piercings, tattoos, man buns, and the like are perfectly acceptable statements of personality, there is nothing personal in business, so consider whether these personal expressions are appropriate and will further your professional goals. Does the boss have a man bun? If not, you should not have one. Dress for the job you want, not for the job you have.

Business casual is the thing now, but you always want to dress slightly better than your coworkers and not be the most casual one there. You can look professional even while wearing neat and pressed business casual clothes. Not overly flashy or sexy unless you are a musician or artist. That does not mean boring, but it does mean tasteful. If you don't know how to do that, then hire Stitch Fix or go to a store with knowledgeable associates who can guide you. Also pay attention to how your boss and other executives dress.

PROTECT YOUR SOCIAL MEDIA.

In today's online culture, most companies check your social media before making an offer of employment. Remember, social media posts have a long life. If you are unhappy with your job and/or your boss, never post these feelings on social media, as your "friends" may pass these posts to your boss. The worst case scenario is forgetting your boss is a Facebook friend and still posting to social media. In either case, you may not have to worry about your job or boss much longer.

PROTECT YOUR CREDIT HISTORY.

Many companies will check your credit history before making an offer of employment, having found there is a correlation between poor credit history and problematic employees. Poor credit history indicates a pattern of irresponsibility that could lead to distracted behavior due to personal finances. In addition, people with poor credit are not generally hired for jobs responsible for cash handling, accounting transactions, or a variety of other job responsibilities. This may not seem fair, but that is the way of the world. Their reasoning? Employees with poor credit history—and possibly problems with their personal finances—may be tempted to steal from the company if the opportunity presents itself. Think of it this way: if the red flag of poor credit history appears, the hiring manager is exposed to criticism if he ignores the red flag and a problem does occur. Why would the hiring manager put himself in that position?

Your life will be much easier and stress free if you understand and work within the system. Fighting the system will wear you out and get you nowhere. Once you make it to the top, feel free to make changes.

NEGOTIATING

Maybe you are a buyer for a retail store, you buy close-out merchandise, or you deal in parts within a manufacturing plant. No matter the job, when negotiating to make a purchase, make the first offer.

Conventional wisdom says that he who makes the first offer loses, but here is the argument for making the first offer—if you are prepared to pay $100, and the seller wants five times that number, the seller cannot—in good faith—say that his item is worth five times your first offer. The seller must now counter with a number that is closer to your first offer.

Note this strategy does not apply to salary negotiations. Each deal may call for a different strategy, so consider the best strategy before negotiating.

When negotiating to purchase a product or service, there are three elements of the deal: quality, speed, and cost. You get to choose two of the three.

NAVIGATING CORPORATE AMERICA II

I met James Loomstein at an SMU seminar, where a young entrepreneur discussed her successful business start-up. James is an adjunct professor at Southern Methodist University Cox School of Business and a sought-after digital marketing speaker. Loomstein has more than fifteen years of experience in strategic planning, digital marketing, and consumer insights. He is a managing partner for Rogue Marketing, specializing in digital marketing. James contributed the following topics during the seminar's lunch break.

GOOD BOSSES

If you have a good boss, count your blessings because there are mediocre or worse bosses in the workplace. Good bosses will support you, recognize your contributions to the organization, protect you (if necessary) from budget cuts and nasty politics, provide constructive criticism, treat you fairly, and motivate you to be the best you can be.

Good leaders are a rare breed, and you should stay connected with them as long as possible. Hopefully, good bosses will take you with them as they grow with the organization. Good bosses may also be good mentors.

JOB LOSS

It is very possible that you will lose your job at some point through no fault of your own. In the '50s through the '80s, employees spent their entire careers at one company like JCPenney, Sears, GE, GM, US Steel, and other large companies. Today, lifetime employment rarely exists. Many companies have their day in the sun and then decline, and this cycle seems to be happening more quickly. Or maybe your company gets a new top executive, and this person wants people that he or she knows and trusts. To drive home this point, the new CEO brings in a new VP of marketing and a new department head. Sometimes, the turnover goes pretty deep. There is a tremendous amount of pressure for top executives to perform, and turnover at the top can occur every two to three years if the company's numbers are not good, or if your company is bought or merged with another company.

I joined a fast-growing retail company, Tuesday Morning, Inc., in the early 1990s as part of an entire department renewal. This company had promised the old department personnel a bright future with hefty pay raises and increased responsibility. They were all terminated as part of the department renewal. In order to qualify for severance, each person was required to train the new personnel. Not a nice thank you for their loyal service and extra effort on nights and weekends. Nevertheless, our new team made the transition and continued to work magic, grow the company, and accomplish the following major initiatives:

- Implemented two new accounting systems

- Refinanced the company's debt
- Took the company private through a leveraged buyout (LBO)
- Took the company public (IPO) eighteen months later.

Each of those initiatives required a tremendous amount of effort on top of our daily duties. Not long after these initiatives were accomplished, a new CEO arrived and wanted an entire department renewal for our group as well as many other departments. Sound familiar? It happens all the time. This renewal gave us a firsthand perspective on what our predecessors had experienced.

Fortunately, we all found better jobs with an increase in salary and the opportunity to share the knowledge and experience we had gained working for Tuesday Morning, Inc. Since the department/company renewal was outside of our control, we all did our best to embrace the uncertain future. Through it all, we had positive attitudes and faith that things would work out in the long run. We all know that change is hard, but it is inevitable. We also know that difficult times present the opportunity to grow stronger.

Stay curious. The world is changing faster than it ever has. Skill sets and education that worked well for the baby boomers may not serve future generations as well. Maybe by taking a quick look at where we came from, you can determine where we are going.

During the industrial revolution—1760 to the mid-1840s—textile machines produced thread and fabric more efficiently. Iron was needed to make these machines and was later used to make metal bridges and the first ships made of riveted iron plates. As a result of the industrial revolution, people began moving off farms and into cities.

From 1840 to 1920, technological progress and economic development created by the industrial revolution continued the economic expansion with improvements in transportation—the creation of trains, steamboats, and automobiles.

After the 1920s, the technological revolution continued with the advent of aviation, space exploration, radio, television, film, telephones, and information technology. It was during this time period that a college degree was the ticket to getting ahead. By the mid-1970s, people were chasing graduate degrees and MBAs for an edge to get ahead. After all, everybody had a college degree. Today, a college degree does not provide the security it once did, particularly if you invest in a major that has little marketable demand.

So where do we go from here? Forecasting is difficult, especially if it is about the future. In other words, I don't have the answer. But I do have some tips that might help no matter the future ahead.

- Be a lifelong learner.
- Be flexible and open to new ideas.
- Embrace change.
- Stay competitive and marketable in our fast-changing environment.
- Stay on your toes and be ready and prepared to move quickly.
- Keep your eyes and ears open for opportunity.

- Read books, magazines, respected internet articles, and think.

- Take advantage of seminars where smart and successful people are making presentations. Also, be sure to network with the attendees. Trade business cards and write a note on the cards you collect to remember how you connected with the individual. You never know when you will need to reach out to other professionals.

- Stay informed about artificial intelligence (AI). AI may be the next game-changer in the continued technological revolution. Is there a career opportunity in AI for you, or is AI coming for your job? If so, better get moving. Don't get caught flat-footed. Be ready.

Will you be creative and adaptive to capitalize on the next big thing? Cornelius Vanderbilt did just that. Cornelius was born in 1794 and started a passenger ferry with one boat in the Hudson River. He grew the ferry business into a large shipping empire and then sold the business, thinking trains would be the next big thing—and they were. In a world of uncertainty, Cornelius was able to see around the corner in order to capitalize on the next big thing. Today, the world is more uncertain and complicated, which means opportunity for the next Cornelius.

Build a large network of friends. One day, you may need to call a friend with a question, and the person will be there for you. I never thought I would write a book, but here I am. I had many questions about the process: where to start, how to find a publisher, an editor, a graphic artist, how much it cost, and so forth. Fortunately, I have several friends who have published books, and they all gave their unique perspective on the process.

Your questions will certainly be different. If you start a business, you might wonder how to raise capital, why you can't get a bank loan, how long a customer should take before remitting payment, what the legal ramifications of X, Y, and Z are, and so on. If you don't start building your network now, you may find yourself with no one to call for that quick but crucial question.

An acquaintance tells a story about his offspring, whose college roommate stiffed her out of the last month of rent in their senior year, and the dispute over the rent became ugly. The family that was stiffed was a well-known and respected family in the region with deep connections in the business community. This is the type of friend who rarely comes into your life and should be preserved as a lifelong friendship. What an unfortunate ending to a friendship and potential lifelong network contact over a month's rent. Do not underestimate the power of all your relationships, only focusing on those that appear on the surface to be business related. All of your relationships are crucial to your career.

The best time to start building your network is while you are in school. Identify those people who appear most likely to succeed and friend them on social media, but, more importantly, in person. How you do this will depend on individual circumstances, but picking the right time is key. Additionally, I suggest a one-on-one conversation. Maybe there is a common thread between you and your target network, such as a study group or an extracurricular activity.

Be a problem solver. In today's world, most of what you

need is available on the internet—just Google it. It is quite different from the baby boomers' world, where school required substantial memorization and instruction on how to do specific tasks without the benefit of a computer. Many baby boomers did not even have the benefit of a calculator and had to use a slide rule! Just imagine what you can learn from people who had to do everything the long, hard way. You won't know until you open a dialogue with the older generation. Do it!

This change represents a huge paradigm shift in the methods and time required to do work and solve problems. Today, one or two people solve problems in an afternoon—versus the old days, when a team of people solicited information from experts in various fields. In order to stand out from your peers, be a problem solver and do things that make life easier for your boss.

- Avoid presenting a problem without also presenting a solution.
- Innovate and offer ideas to reduce costs or increase sales.
- Be early.
- Work hard and always present a positive attitude.
- Do what it takes to get the job done without complaining.
- Be supportive of your boss.
- Exceed your goals.
- Try hard to minimize mistakes, but always learn from them.

PART IV
CHANGING JOBS

LEAVING A JOB

When the job market is hot, you may receive a job offer that you cannot refuse. Or you might receive a job offer to escape from an unhappy job situation. In either situation, it is important to leave your current job with grace.

You never know when you will need a reference or a kind word from your past employer or coworker. Be professional. Your boss should be the first to know either through a face-to-face meeting or Zoom call. As tempting as it may be, never discuss your planned departure with your coworkers before discussing it with your boss, as this may result in your boss learning about your departure from the rumor mill. If this happens, it will be embarrassing to your manager and could impact any future reference or kind words they could have had for you if you'd shown them that respect.

As part of the discussion with your supervisor, agree on how to announce your departure, especially if you have people that report to you.

Advice for resignation letters:

- Keep it simple, maybe only a few sentences.

- Never be negative—again, think about future references.

- Address the letter to your supervisor.

- Include notice of your last day, which should be at least two weeks away. Two weeks is an industry standard, but your new employer may need you sooner, or your old employer may prefer a longer transition period. These issues will need to be discussed to agree on the best transition for all.

- Know that once the letter is delivered, your decision to leave is irrefutable.

- If sincerity permits, express gratitude for the opportunity to work with the company as well as for all that you have learned.

During your transition from your old company, don't slack off. You want to leave on a high note, with positive feelings from your supervisor and coworkers. Goodbyes should be short and positive. Be happy, but not excessively happy (e.g., don't rub it in people's faces that you are leaving). It can feel very personal to leave coworkers and supervisors who you've known for some time and seen for many hours during the week, but they are still running a business and should not be impacted by a distraction that affects performance and/or quality.

Just as important, if not more so—don't burn bridges. You never know what the future will hold, nor how people from your last company may cross paths with you again.

I had a friend who worked for a fast-growing company but became dissatisfied with the management team. He soon left the company to work for a competitor. Six months later, his old company purchased his new company.

Fortunately, he had left on good terms, and he kept his job after the acquisition.

On the other side of the coin, an acquaintance was terminated after a long tenure with a company that was going through some tough financial times and downsizing a large part of the workforce. My acquaintance spoke harshly about his company to friends—and anyone who would listen—and also posted harsh words on Facebook. The result was that he was blacklisted in the business community. Not good when you have a family to support.

Most companies will check your social media before making an offer, so long before you plan to join the permanent workforce, consider the impact that today's social media post may have on tomorrow's job search. The best indicator of future behavior is past behavior, so why would a new company hire you if they see you bashing another company? You're only going to feel that way temporarily, until you move on to bigger and better things, but speaking those temporary feelings aloud will certainly follow you for a very long time.

I live in the Dallas-Fort Worth metroplex, which has a population of 6.5 million. Although a big city, it is a small town when you consider individual professional groups. Everyone in the professional groups seems to know each other or someone in the metroplex's companies. It's not much different in other cities and other industries—nationwide or even worldwide—especially with social media being such a direct and quick way to spread gossip. And don't forget, your underling could be your boss tomorrow. The takeaway is to always be professional and never burn bridges.

Conducting a Job Searching While Still Employed—

Your chances of landing a job when you have a job are much better than if you are unemployed. Companies want to hire the best and conventional wisdom says that the best of the best are usually employed. If you do not have a job, it raises questions in the prospective employer's mind. So it is never a good idea to quit your current job before searching for a new job. Additionally, if you are without a current job, you are in a significantly weaker position where you might settle on a so-so job due to the fact that you need a job.

When looking for a job while you already have a job, care must be taken to avoid some not so obvious landmines which mostly relate to confidentiality. You do not want your boss to find out that you are looking for a job as he or she may take it personally which could make your life uncomfortable or—even worse—result in your termination. To help ensure that your boss does not know about your job search before you submit your resignation letter:

- Do not tell any of your coworkers or anyone else at your company about your job search. If you do, gossip and the grapevine may rat you out. And, of course, never mention your job search on social media.

- Your prospective employer should be told that your job search is confidential.

- Do not use current coworkers or supervisors as references.

- Do not schedule interviews during work hours. Not only will this help in the area of confidentiality, it will help ensure you are focused and committed to your current job.

- Do not use company resources in your job search, including the following:

    — Your computer—you never know when you are being watched either physically or electronically.

    — Internet—many companies track employee usage looking for noncompany-related usage.

    — Phone—you may be overheard having a conversation with your prospective employer at the worst possible moment.

    — Copy machine—someone may walk up and see what you are copying or you may accidentally leave confidential documents on the copier.

- Do not post your resume on job boards, as your current employer may see it. However, you should keep your LinkedIn profile current and accurate. Many people do this, and so it should not raise suspicion. In addition, a prospective employer may be interested in your LinkedIn profile and contact you. However, it should go without saying that your LinkedIn profile should not indicate that you are looking for new opportunities.

- After adhering to the above, don't blow your cover by wearing a suit and tie to work when you usually wear jeans. Bring your interview clothes to work and change offsite.[24]

---

24 Jacquelyn Smith, "The Dos and Don'ts of Job Searching while You're Still Employed," Forbes, October 26, 2012, www.forbes.com/sites/jacquelynsmith/2012/10/26/the-dos-and-donts-of-job-searching-while-youre-still-employed/?sh=22ee8baa7e07.

If you are unhappy in your job and think it is time for a new job, think deeply about why you are unhappy and if there are things you like about your current situation. A yes-or-no approach to your issues may reveal it is time to leave, or you may surprise yourself with the realization that you are happier than you thought. Before completing this exercise, it will be necessary to weight the issues, especially if the yes's and no's are evenly balanced. Use a grid like this to rank your priorities, and then indicate yes or no for your happiness in each area.

	WEIGHT (high or low?)	YES	NO
I am unhappy because _____ (e.g., my boss is micromanaging me).			
The work is boring, tedious, too much volume, or not the right job for me.			
I am no longer learning and not being promoted.			
People issues—coworkers or boss			
Discrimination, harassment, or unfair treatment			
Stress			
Salary issues			
Recognition issues			
Add other pros and cons that come to mind			

Changing jobs, a cautionary note—When Kevin O'Leary of *Shark Tank* fame sees an applicant's resume with multiple jobs over the past years, he puts it in the garbage. He says that companies don't like to invest in people who change jobs frequently due to the hiring expenses. These expenses include onboarding, training, lost productivity, and possibly sending equipment to remote workers. Why hire someone if they appear likely to leave in a few months? He recommends that employees have at least a two-year mental commitment, whether or not they like the job.[25]

If you stuck around longer in previous jobs, this gives you some flexibility if you have subsequent jobs that lasted less than two years.

---

25 "When Kevin O'Leary Sees This Resume Red Flag, 'I Simply Put It into the Garbage,'" www.msn.com/en-us/money/careersandeducation/when-kevin-o-leary-sees-this-resume-red-flag-i-simply-put-it-into-the-garbage/ar-AAQkpmB?ocid=msedgntp.

WHEN CAREER PLANS ARE DERAILED

IN 2020, THE COVID-19 PANDEMIC dominated headlines worldwide. Hopefully, all of that will be in our rear-view mirror by the time you read this. However, over the course of your professional career, there will be ups and downs as a result of big impacts on society in general, as there have been for every generation before yours. This chapter addresses what to do if your career plans are derailed due to a fundamental change in the economy.

In February 2020, the economy was humming. Unemployment rates were low, employers were competing for employees, and the stock market was at a record high. Then, in March, stay-at-home and shelter-in-place federal, state, and county orders became the new normal. Unemployment rates shot up to historic highs while the stock market dropped 30-plus percent.

Throughout this process, there was a tremendous amount of suffering. I read about people of all income categories being food insecure and losing their homes due to foreclosures and "mean" landlords forcing renters out. Of course, most of the suffering was at the lower-income levels, but many people—including upper-income families—live beyond their means, so when upper-income families experienced a job loss, they had a long way to fall due to unsustainable/large mortgages and car, boat, and credit card payments, etc. I also read about college graduates relying on the strong economy to find jobs with nonspecific/nonmarketable degrees.

There are steps you can take to improve your situation in times like the COVID pandemic of 2020. My mantra is "Timing is everything." I graduated in the mid-1970s, when the job market was dismal due to persistent high inflation and stagnant demand in the economy, which was known as stagflation. I found a twelve-month MBA program that helped me move forward and be productive until the job market improved, and it worked. You may not be able to find your dream job during times like that, but you can always find ways to be productive and improve yourself.

Do not sit in your parents' basement playing video games until the economy improves. Doing so will negatively impact your future prospects as well as your motivation. You must push forward to improve yourself in your vocation of choice—or to assume a temporary vocation change that will position you to earn where the demand may be at that time.

Some food for thought to improve yourself and your marketability:

- If you are a casual user of Excel, study to become a power user who is proficient with Pivot Tables, VLOOKUP, graphs, if/then statements, and all the bells and whistles that go with each. **Consider Excel University,** which provides beginning, intermediate, and advanced Excel classes online. https://www.excel-university.com

- If you are a casual user of Word, study to become a power user who is proficient with tables, formatting, pulling data from Excel spreadsheets, mail merge, etc. and all the bells and whistles that go with each.

- If you are interested in engineering or manufacturing, take a CAD (computer-aided design) course.

- Take a computer graphics course if you are interested in marketing.

- Take a public speaking course, which will improve your speaking skills for most careers.

- Check out what types of online self-study or educational material from Amazon's bookstore might benefit you.

- Learn or improve your foreign language skills.

- Take an online class or courses toward a degree.

- Apply for technical training. Maybe you always wanted to weld or be an HVAC technician or an electrician.

- Ask potential employers what type of study they recommend you pursue to enhance your skills during the downtime.

By improving yourself while the economy recovers, you will be able to answer potential employers' question when they ask what you did during the lockdown and/or economic recovery period. Hopefully, your answer will impress the interviewer. Telling the interviewer that you played video games in your parents' basement will not.

In addition to the derailment of career plans, life does not always unfold as planned. There will be many small and large ups and downs in life, and your reaction to these changes will determine the outcome.

When things happen such as the loss of a loved one, loss of a job, or not getting that longed-for promotion, you may experience a major transition. Life constantly throws curveballs. Expect them, and be flexible and adaptable. Stay centered, and don't make changes impulsively. Think it through. Act, don't *re*act. Most, if not all, trauma and drama that you experience in your personal, professional, and financial life will dissipate over time and look small in your rear-view mirror.

Also, keep in mind that your logical self may understand and accept the curveballs, but your emotional self may not. To be at peace, your logical and emotional selves need to be in agreement. Sometimes this will happen over time, and sometimes you may have trouble adjusting and need help reconciling your two selves. Don't hesitate to seek out a professional counselor to help you through and get you on your feet again. This is money well spent.

Some relevant quotes from graduation speeches follow:

They say everything happens for a reason. I don't know if that's true, but I do know everything happens, and it's up to you to maximize the reality of your situation.

—Ken Jeong, stand-up comedian, actor, and former physician (University of North Carolina, Greensboro, commencement speech, May 2019)

It is impossible to live without failing at something, unless you live so cautiously that you might as well not have lived at all—in which case, you fail by default.... The knowledge that you have emerged wiser and stronger from setbacks means that you are, ever after, secure in your ability to survive. You will never truly know yourself, or the strength of your relationships, until both have been tested by adversity.

> —Author J. K. Rowling (Harvard University commencement speech, 2008)

If you love only yourself, you will serve only yourself. And you will have only yourself. So no more winning. Instead, try to love others and serve others, and hopefully find those who love and serve you in return.

> —Stephen Colbert, comedian (Northwestern University commencement speech, 2011)

There's a difference between gifts and choices. Cleverness is a gift; kindness is a choice.

> —Jeff Bezos, founder, CEO, and president of Amazon.com, Inc. (Princeton commencement speech, 2010)

NAVIGATING CORPORATE AMERICA III

HUMAN RESOURCES (HR) FRIEND OR FOE?

HR WALKS A FINE LINE between protecting the company and handling employee complaints from a variety of departments. Companies have multiple departments, all of which are important. Some departments are the engines to grow the top and bottom lines of the profit-and-loss statement, while other departments are considered support or administrative overhead. Though all departments have the opportunity to reduce cost, the departments that are the engines for growth and profit are "kings" within the four corporate walls.

The CEO lives, breathes, and believes this hierarchy and lavishes support, praise, and resources on the kings. Of course, if the kings don't meet high performance goals, they are quietly fired. Growth-engine departments include the sales and marketing departments, and in a retail organization, the kings are the buyers.

Each industry may have different departments that are considered kings. For example, engineers/programmers are the kings in technology companies. There are other departments that play key roles, such as operations and supply chain. While these departments are not drivers of revenue and profits, they are incredibly important to the operation of the organization. Generally, the administrative overhead departments include accounting, HR, real estate, and loss prevention.

No one is above the "law" and, for example, racist or sexist actions are not tolerated. As a nation, this statement holds more and more "truthiness." But in reality, the kings get special treatment up and until their actions are egregious. I have seen it, and I have heard special treatments verbalized. Corporate law is not applied equally.

Maybe you have read or watched the news when a king is fired and/or prosecuted for racist or sexist actions. How long had these actions been taking place before there were consequences? Often, the answer is years, not weeks or months, AND the improper actions were generally well known before action was finally taken.

Separate treatment is wrong and certainly not fair, but we live in an imperfect world. One of my coworkers often said, as it relates to fair, "The fair only comes once a year."

- *Here's the bottom line*—if you have a run-in with one of the kings of the company who is abusive or otherwise out of line, the offense must be incredibly extreme for disciplinary action of the offending king. This is especially true if this king is the king of kings, the best of the best. This is obviously not fair, but it's something you need to be aware of as you enter the world of work. Don't poke the bear!

ADMINISTRATIVE OVERHEAD DEPARTMENTS

Let's take a closer look at one of the administrative overhead departments: the accounting department. Unless your firm is a

CPA firm where accounting is your business, the CEO is often comparing the cost of the accounting department to that of the competition in order to cram down cost reductions.

Over the years, technology has reduced the accounting department's staffing needs and improved their speed and accuracy and will continue to do so. But technology comes at a price to purchase, install, and to train the staff. Senior management wants the benefits of the technology but not the associated cost. Some CEOs even go as far as to ask why the accounting department or any other support function department is needed. This type of inquiry makes me wonder about senior management's understanding and suitability for their jobs.

A couple of examples highlight this concern.

- One company was in the process of installing a complex accounting/ERP software package. The difficult installation, performed by a third party, resulted in cost overruns as well as time delays due to the complexity of the software. Frustrated with the cost overruns and time delays, and against the advice of the third-party installer and the accounting department, the CEO insisted that the new software be immediately turned on. Shortly after the new system was turned on, the company realized that the system was not billing for merchandise sales. Unable to go back to the old system and unable to quickly correct this large hole in the new system, the company declared bankruptcy.

- Another major retailer felt that it could save money by hiring people without the CPA designation and/

or an accounting background into their accounting department. Within a year of this policy change, the accounting records were in such a mess that most of the accounting staff was fired and replaced with people with accounting backgrounds and/or CPAs.

So what's the point, and what does this mean to you?

- Senior management is reluctant to spend scarce resources on projects, assets, or staffing that do not increase the top or bottom lines. That is, support function departments are the redheaded stepchildren. In addition, senior management has little tolerance for delays in project rollouts, and they frequently make fatal mistakes due to this frustration. Fatal mistakes rarely happen with the departments run by the kings, because senior management has a better understanding of the issues and will always take the time to ensure understanding before making a rash and fatal mistake.

- Human nature is tough to change. Senior management is inclined to align resources with those departments that generate revenue and profit at the expense of administrative overhead departments. This might explain why members of the accounting department are often the first to arrive in the morning and the last to leave at the end of the day (a sign that they are understaffed).

PART V
IMPORTANT GENERAL CONCEPTS

DOS AND DON'TS

You only have to do a very few things right in your life so long as you don't do too many things wrong.

—Warren Buffett[26]

- Do send a thank-you note after job interviews. This will set you apart from the competition. Be sure to consider the age range of your interviewer and use appropriate digital or written methods accordingly.

- Do research typical interview questions and practice your answers before going to an interview. Being prepared will show in your answers as well as in how confident you appear.

- Do have an answer for "Where do you see yourself in five years?" Employers prefer candidates with vision and the ability to effectively communicate that vision, in addition to wanting to know their investment in training you won't be quickly lost.

- Don't bad-mouth your former boss. If you bad-mouth your former boss in an interview

---

26 "Warren Buffett," 2020, https://www.azquotes.com/quote/40650.

situation, the interviewer will probably wonder what will happen if you don't like him or her. Stay professional.

- Don't criticize or make fun of your colleagues because it will probably get back to them and damage your influence.[27]

- Do ensure that your computer requires a password if you are away from your workstation. Also, protect your passwords. You do not want the office jokester sending inappropriate emails under your name or an outsider accessing company files.

- Don't snoop in coworkers' workstations or computers.

- Don't open anyone else's notepads or files without permission.

- Don't steal your coworkers' food.

- Do your best no matter how menial the task! In the competitive world we live in, strive to be outstanding and enthusiastic about all assignments.[28]

- Do work hard and work smart. People who don't

---

[27] Ben Carpenter, The Bigs: The Secrets Nobody Tells Students and Young Professionals about How to Find a Great Job, Do a Great Job, Be a Leader, Start a Business, Stay Out of Trouble, and Live A Happy Life (Wiley 2014).

[28] Ben Carpenter, The Bigs: The Secrets Nobody Tells Students and Young Professionals about How to Find a Great Job, Do a Great Job, Be a Leader, Start a Business, Stay Out of Trouble, and Live A Happy Life, (Wiley 2014).

work hard may think the other guy is just lucky. Maybe luck plays a part, but hard work is more likely the cause of their luck. The harder you pull, the easier it will come.

- Do ensure you have a positive relationship with your boss. Nothing outside of your work performance, attitude, and capacity to learn is more important. Having a strong and positive relationship with your coworkers is a close second.

- Don't use throwaway lines on the phone or in emails, as they are unnecessary and do not project a professional image.

  — When answering the phone, answer with your name—versus your name plus "May I help you?"

  — When closing out an email, don't say, "Let me know if you have any questions." The recipient will ask questions, so there is no need to tell them what to do.

- Don't ignore your company's policy on cell phone use and especially don't check your cell phone during meetings.

- Do take your vacation. If your company has a use-it-or-lose-it policy, don't lose it! Do get a reasonable amount of sleep and exercise regularly. There will be plenty of time to party on the weekends, but your top priority has to be your job.

- Don't drink and drive—a DWI may keep you from getting your next job.

- Do join Toastmasters (https://www.toastmasters.org/). This is a great way to improve your speaking skills and confidence in speaking to groups. Lessons learned from Toastmasters will pay dividends throughout your career.

- Do stay positive and stay away from those who complain.

- Do think before you act or speak. Remember to act, never react.

- Don't say, "No problem." Say, "You're welcome," "My pleasure," or "Happy to do it." "Problem" is a negative word, while the other choices more clearly convey a positive attitude.

- Do keep your reporting manager in the loop.

- Do choose your friends wisely and carefully. During your formative years, friends have a huge impact on your future. Pick friends who appear to share similar goals. You might be drawn to or intrigued by goths, gamers, gangs, or you name it. If this is not how you see yourself five to ten years down the road, resist the temptation.

- Don't get into an intimate relationship at work. It almost always leads to disaster. Though it can be hard to abide by, personal friendships and relationships should only exist outside of work.

- Do bring a notepad and pen to meetings and be a couple of minutes early.

- Do communicate bad news to your supervisor quickly. Examples include the following: we have been hacked; some accounting files were accidentally deleted; one of the numbers in the month-end closing report is in error; we cannot submit the payroll file to the processor; and the advertising campaign does not appear to be working.

- Do identify those coworkers moving up in the organization and try to understand why they have succeeded. Always be on the watch for examples of the success you are seeking and learn from them.

- Do read and continue to learn with a growth mindset. Learn new skills, take night courses, or obtain your degree while working a full-time job. I have known several people who earned advanced degrees while working their full-time jobs by committing nights and weekends to their quests. They earned the respect of family, friends, and coworkers, and ultimately, they received desired promotions.

- Don't be someone people think of as a know-it-all. Be respectful and kind when you help others learn and grow.

- Do embrace change—it is inevitable.

- Do accept responsibility for your failures and make it a point to learn from them.

- Do show gratitude rather than a sense of entitlement.
- Do Google "successful people" to obtain insight into their traits.
- Do be prepared to work for your paycheck!
- Do say goodnight to your coworkers and supervisors. Don't just get up and leave. Ask your supervisor if he or she needs anything before you leave.
- Don't call in sick when you are not sick.
- Don't involve yourself in office gossip.
- Don't discuss confidential matters outside of the inner circle of confidentiality. Discussing merger and acquisition plans, salary data, planned terminations, store closings, and so forth outside of the inner circle of confidentiality can get you fired.
- Don't spend your productive years backpacking through Europe or on a sabbatical. When you return from your travels and are ready to enter or reenter the workforce, expect that a prospective employer will ask what you have been doing over the past three to five years. If you have not been motivated to work and move your career forward consistently, without gaps, many employers will see that as a lack of motivation and will not be inclined to hire you.
- Do work hard and work smart. Check and double-check to ensure your work is free of errors. Companies already have a recipe for success by the

time you join their team. Follow and/or exceed all steps in the recipe and don't cut corners.

- When at company social events such as Christmas parties, picnics, golf outings, client dinners, off-site meetings, seminars, or conventions, your actions are being watched. Things to avoid include the following:

  — Heavy drinking

  — Late morning arrivals due to late evenings

  — Sleeping during seminars or convention sessions

  — Getting drunk on the golf course and driving your golf cart onto the green of your boss's country club—this will get you fired!

  — Sleeping around with company personnel. Do you want a career or a good time? It can't be both.

- Do ensure that you have a basic understanding of Microsoft Office before entering the workforce; otherwise, you will be at a huge disadvantage against your peers.

- Don't be petty. I had an employee who submitted an expense report that included travel items, a fee for a professional certification, and the cost of a postage stamp to mail the certification renewal. I thought the request for reimbursement of the $0.29 stamp petty and would reflect poorly on my department. I refused to sign the expense report unless the postage stamp was removed. This employee argued the point but did submit a revised expense report. My professional and personal opinion of this individual was never the same.

- A short intro is needed before these don'ts. A buddy of mine owns a business buying and selling leather around the world. He is a baby boomer, and one of his employees is a millennial. Together, they are like oil and water. They do not mix. Some of the don'ts for this millennial are as follows:

  — If you work late, do not come in late thinking that the two balance out.

  — If you work Saturday, do not assume that you can take Monday off.

  — If you are a salaried employee, working a few extra hours does not excuse you from being present during normal business hours unless your boss gives you prior approval. Some millennials may feel that these actions are acceptable; a baby boomer boss may disagree. There are two rules as it applies to the boss that helped me over the years. Rule number one, the boss is always right. Rule number two, if the boss is wrong, refer to rule number one. If and when you have a millennial boss, your work habits may better align.

  — If you are new, don't try to be an expert around

the experts. Listen and learn with respect to those who built the company that offered you a job. Build your reputation, and then suggest changes on all the information available and a reputation that will make them interested in listening to you.

— If you ask why you have not been promoted, do not get mad when you are given several reasons. Your boss is taking his time to honestly explain his reasons. You should express your appreciation for the straightforward explanation, which can benefit you as a developmental opportunity.

THINGS THAT MATTER

Remember: The things that don't matter, don't matter.

Save as much as you can for as long as you can as soon as you can, and always spend less than you have coming in, forever. This alone will keep you financially secure!

Modern Slaves are Not in Chains; they are in Debt.

—Unknown

Everything you've ever wanted is on the other side of fear.

— George Adair, well-known speaker, philosopher, and author.

Amateurs practice until they can get it right; professionals practice until they can't get it wrong.

—Harold Craxton, former professor at the Royal Academy of Music (Aug 29, 2013)

THREE THINGS TO KNOW AS YOU GROW

GETTING OLDER HAS ITS ADVANTAGES. Each day you live, you understand more about how the world actually works and are able to connect dots you never thought belonged. You will know your strengths and know what to improve upon. Of course, there are some downsides. Responsibilities pile up, and you will begin to collect doctors. That's okay. Priorities change.

Growing up often results in outgrowing relationships. You probably share interests and priorities with your friends until your mid-twenties, but after that, some things change. Young people have a common bond of growing and developing, but once their lives take on a specific direction such as career, marriage, children, and so on, things change, which can result in outgrowing relationships. This is normal and can impact both social and romantic relationships.

Give yourself permission to fail. Failure is a part of life. Give yourself permission to fail; otherwise, you may stay in your comfort zone and not experience bold or radically different opportunities. There is no such thing as perfection, and setting unachievable goals will only hold you back from reaching your true, imperfect yet awesome potential. Failure is often a learning opportunity, so do not give up. We learn more from our mistakes than from our successes. Keep learning and keep swinging for the fences. That's what life is about, the journey and the experiences. Fear of failure can hold you back from many things that can change your life for the better. If you fail, time will heal your wounds, but the growth from your experience is worth the temporary grief.

Sometimes you win, sometimes you learn.

—John Maxwell

But my fear of failure never approached in magnitude my fear of what if.... For many of you who maybe don't have it all figured out, it's okay....Enjoy the process of your search without succumbing to the pressure of the result. Trust your gut. Keep throwing darts at the dartboard. Don't listen to the critics and you will figure it out.

—Will Ferrell, comedian (USC commencement speech, 2017)

Focus on life's experiences and the journey and not on material things. When you look back on your life so far, you probably have a stronger memory of relationships, family time, trips, and friends than material things. So focus on memories, not on material things. Material things do not guarantee happiness, and happiness does not require material things.

ONLINE MEETING AND COLLABORATING ETIQUETTE

COVID SPARKED A SPEED UP of society using virtual tools. Virtual functionality is probably a trend that will continue for quite some time. As a society, we will need to adapt to technology as well as the etiquette for using this new technology.

Whenever there is a massive shift in the way we live, processes will and must change. Seismic change is an opportunity that rarely comes along. Ups and downs and paradigm shifts are a natural part of the life. These things do not necessarily happen frequently or on a regular basis, so when they do happen, it creates disruption and disruption created opportunity. COVID is the most recent example that created the need for processes, procedures, and computer applications to support social distancing. A few of the technological changes to support the change that COVID brought into our life follow.

- Zoom/Microsoft Teams
- DocuSign
- Touchless technologies of all kinds

- App/online ordering to enhance social distancing as well as to reduce order-taking personnel needs, which enables a higher hourly wage for the remaining personnel
- Amazon grocery grab and go
- Online shopping for groceries with quick delivery or curbside pickup
- Greater adoption of Apple Pay and PayPal
- Microsoft and Apple technology enhancements to improve productivity during social distancing.

What will the next shift demand or facilitate? As of the writing of this book, Facebook announced a name change to Meta Platforms and a rebranding of their focus to bring us even more advanced online abilities, including attending events/meetings that include holograms.

What's next? When change occurs, think deeply about how you and your company can quickly adapt. Seize the opportunity to develop technologies, processes, and products to deal with this change, and you may be handsomely rewarded.

Until sometime in 2020, it was rare to have video meetings, now mostly referred to as Zoom meetings. Some may have thought that working from home would put an end to the dreaded office meeting. Far from it! As we began using this new technology, many of us made Zoom meeting etiquette mistakes. So if you are new to Zoom business meetings, the following is a list of etiquette for your consideration.

- Don't be late to your Zoom meeting

- To maximize your image:

  - Use the video option and preview/adjust the position of your camera and lighting in the room if necessary.

  - Stage your background. Make sure your camera view does not include a sink full of dirty dishes or an unmade bed.

  - Look into the camera to give the appearance of eye contact.

- Think through technical issues before you start. Test both audio and video before the meeting begins. When possible, use a wire connection to help ensure audio and video do not freeze. This is especially important when you are sharing your Wi-Fi with someone who is streaming. Use a headset with a microphone to ensure that your voice is at a constant level and distance from the microphone.

- Dress for the job. Don't wear your pajamas.

- Mute your microphone when not speaking to help keep background noise to a minimum.

- Limit distractions. Don't eat during the meeting or do things of a personal nature like picking your nose or going to the bathroom while thinking that the video and microphone are off. If seen or heard by other Zoom attendees, these actions have a long and embarrassing life. Don't laugh; these things have happened.

- Avoid multitasking, such as answering emails and texts.

- Prepare materials in advance.

- The host should be the last one to leave the meeting to ensure no one gets cut off.

DINING ETIQUETTE

Trey Knapp, VP Finance at Sewell Automotive Companies, suggested that I include a dining etiquette chapter because many young jobseekers lack polish in formal business dining situations—not because of crudeness or impoliteness, but out of an innocent lack of knowledge. In any event, you should know which bread plate and water glass is yours, which forks to use in which situation, that unlimited dinner alcohol comes at a cost, and how to avoid embarrassing snafus.

When I was interviewing, fresh out of college, I was often taken out to lunch as part of the process. The purpose of the lunch was to get to know me in a relaxed environment and determine whether I could be trusted to have lunch or dinner with a client without embarrassing my boss or the company.

The interview lunch is a business lunch, so prepare to answer questions and listen. An occasional question from you is important, so be prepared with thoughtful questions. Also, remember that you and the people from your potential new company come from different worlds. You are fresh out of school, and they have been in the workplace for two-plus years. So they will not be impressed with talk of your rowdy, off-the-hook keg party, pool party, or bar hookups. Be cool and learn to adapt to the situation.

Dining etiquette is serious stuff. If you do *not* have good dining etiquette, it will be obvious and could cost you a job.[29]

- Which utensil to use for each course—A typical rule of thumb is to start with the utensil that is farthest from your plate and work your way toward the center of your place setting. Use your utensils for eating, not gesturing, and do not lick your utensils, especially your knife. Your bread plate is to your upper left, and wine and water glasses are to your upper right.

- How to hold your fork:

    — American Style—Hold your fork like a pencil, not like a shovel.

    — Continental Style—Hold fork in the left hand, tines downward.

- Do not talk with your mouth full, even if someone asks you a question; wait until you swallow before answering—taking small bites will help. Do not rock the table with your elbows. Keep your elbows off the table. Rest the hand you are not using in your lap. Do not interfere with other diners' experiences

---

29 Debby Mayne, "Table Manners and Dining Etiquette," The Spruce, updated on March 4, 2020, https://www.thespruce.com/table-manners-and-dining-etiquette-1216971.

by displaying improper etiquette; avoid burping or making other rude sounds at the table.

- Even if you don't follow the beliefs of the prayer, show respect and be silent. If the host offers a toast, lift your glass. It is not necessary to "clink" someone else's glass.

- Place your napkin in your lap and keep it there until you are finished eating. If you must get up at any time during the meal and plan to return, place the napkin on either side of your plate. When you are finished, place your partially folded napkin on the table to the left of your plate.

- Do not order the most expensive item on the menu. Why not? Because it sends the wrong impression about you. You don't want to be perceived as someone who takes advantage of a free meal. Remember, it's all about the impression you create, not the meal. Also, skip any meals that might splash on your tie, even if spaghetti and marinara sauce is your favorite.

- If you are eating out, wait until all the members of your group have been served before picking up your fork. However, if you are at a buffet, you may start when there are others seated at your table.

- Never reach across the table for anything. Instead, ask that condiments be passed from the person closest to the item. Salt and pepper should be passed together. Always use serving utensils and not your own cutlery to lift food from the serving dish.

- Turn off your cell phone before sitting down. It is rude to talk on your phone or text while in the company of others. Keep your phone, keys, and other belongings off the table.

- Taste your food before adding salt, pepper, or other seasoning. If you are dining with a prospective employer, the person may perceive you as someone who acts without knowing the facts. Legend has it that Mr. J. C. Penney did not hire a manager because he added salt and pepper before tasting his food.

- Don't cut all your food before you begin eating. Cut one or two bites at a time.

- Never blow on your food. If it is hot, wait a few minutes for it to cool off.

- If you are drinking from a stemmed glass, hold it by the stem.

- Break your bread into bite-sized pieces, and butter only one bite at a time. If a bread knife is provided (they do this at Outback as well as other restaurants), use the bread knife to place butter on your plate, then use your butter knife (if available) to butter your bread.

- Eat slowly, and pace yourself to finish at the same approximate time as the host or hostess.

- Never use a toothpick or dental floss at the table.

- You may reapply your lipstick, but don't freshen the rest of your makeup at the table.

- Treat the waitstaff with respect; never be rude or condescending to people who serve you food. Or, more globally, treat everyone with respect.

If you are dining in a work-related situation, it's about the work. The impression you make either for getting a job or doing your job should be the focus. There is nothing wrong with eating before or after that lunch or dinner appointment so you can accomplish that well. In a related situation, I knew a super salesman who often took two sets of clients to dinner on many evenings—an early dinner and a late dinner. To fit in with the dinner meetings, he always ordered an entree, but rarely finished his meal so that he could focus on the sales aspect of the meal.

WE ARE A WORK IN PROGRESS

Are you a different person from the person you were ten years ago? Most people would answer yes. Will you be a different person ten years from now? Again, highly likely?

Human Beings are a Work in Progress that mistakenly think they are finished.

—Dr. Dan Gilbert

People may ask you what you want to do/be in five years. Maybe you have an answer. Regardless, it is important to be a lifelong learner, listen to others, and network. Think about the truly great people who have made significant contributions in industry, politics, art, and even great orators and leaders. Most, if not all, honed their skills and knowledge by being lifelong learners and listening to others.

It is highly unlikely that anyone will realize their highest potential in isolation. Seemingly unrelated issues can be joined together for huge gain. As an example, Steve Jobs, cofounder of Apple, Inc., dropped out of college in the mid-seventies and took a calligraphy class. Steve was interested in calligraphy even though it had no practical application in his life at the time. But when the first Macintosh computer was released in 1984, Jobs did something unprecedented and provided a variety of fonts for users. Fonts, as they relate to computers, were seemingly unrelated at the time, but today they are both important and standard functionality.

Steve Jobs was not a computer guy; he was the visionary and marketing genius behind Apple. Steve Wozniak, cofounder of Apple, Inc., was the computer genius behind Apple. Apple might not have been in existence if the two Steves had not collaborated. Steve Jobs started Apple computer after Steve Wozniak, a buddy, showed him a primitive computer he was working on with his computer club. To Steve Wozniak, the computer was a hobby, but Steve Jobs had a vision for this new computer, and the rest is history.

You may not be able to do it alone, and you may not even know what the "it" is until you listen to other people. With people who bring different expertise to the table, you may be able to piece disparate information together to produce something new and extraordinary.

Larry King interviewed over thirty thousand guests during his TV and radio career before he passed away in 2021. He gained a lot of wisdom, and one of Larry's lessons was as follows. "I remind myself every morning: Nothing I say this day will teach me anything. So if I'm going to learn, I must do it by listening."

This book refers many times to being a lifelong learner. Listening to others through networking, seminars, and classes increases your chances of unlocking huge potential in some combination of ideas, thoughts, or disciplines that have not yet been discovered. All of a sudden you have an epiphany. Maybe your epiphany will occur immediately or even years down the road as it did with Steve Jobs and computer fonts. A lifetime commitment to learning and listening to others (networking) will help maximize your chances of success in the business world as well as helping you realize your highest potential.

Cornelius Vanderbilt, previously mentioned in the chapter "Navigating Corporate America II," sold his vast shipping business to invest in railroads. Some thought he had lost his mind at the time, but this daring move turned out to be brilliant in terms of connecting the United States in order to move both freight and people. No doubt he had insight into the future of railroads by being curious, watching and reading about the fledgling industry, and by talking to people in the business.

Many captains of industries were smart and unyielding in their drive and vision, but they did not build their companies alone. The world is more complicated than it was one or two hundred years ago, and it is less likely that a tinkerer will build, create, or invent something that has the kind of impact that Oliver Winchester had with the Winchester repeating rifle. That is not to say that it cannot or will not happen.

The point is, in this complicated and connected world, creating something new, and/or a paradigm shift in the way we think and do things, probably requires collaboration and input from a variety of sources. That is why it is so important to expand your circle of professional and social contacts by networking. As a networker, it is essential to spend time around smart people and to listen and ask questions. Some of the benefits:

- Being exposed to lots of pieces of information or puzzle pieces that may seem unrelated, but, one day, you may fit the puzzle pieces together and create an amazing product or service.

- Having a contact to call when you have an important question. I have a colleague who constantly networks. He is continuously looking for the best practices. He regularly asks his competitors what systems—as well as what processes—they use to manage their businesses.

- Meeting people that may offer you a job or even your dream job.

- Learning lots of interesting information that may be useful in your professional, personal, or financial life.

- Feeling good about yourself for reading, learning, and/or interacting with others and developing your networking and social skills.

- Identifying what type of job, career, or industry appeals to you.

- Identifying a mentor.

- Building a network of long-lasting relationships.

We've covered essential tools that are rarely discussed in college. Choose and select the tools that fit your situation and keep focused on your career path.

> *"Too soon, we're old. Too late, we're smart."*
>
> —Old proverb, source unknown

What can you do about getting old too soon? Other than use the time you have wisely, probably nothing. Don't postpone those things you can do now until later. As you get older, you don't have the vigor, physical fitness, and desire of a young person. So if you want to travel or start a physical activity like sailing or board surfing, do it sooner rather than later. Develop and gather interests and hobbies while you are young. Your old self will be most appreciative.

What can you do about getting smart too late? Recognize that you don't know what you don't know, and avail yourself of every opportunity to learn. Read, take classes, and listen to people who are well-informed or have specific knowledge.

Young people tend to overestimate their knowledge of the world and how it works—or how it should work—and underestimate the value of seeking wisdom from generations before them. In reality, we gain wisdom and understanding over years of experience. If this is true, and I believe it to be so, we should take every advantage to gain knowledge sooner rather than later, and that is the impetus of this book.

I hope you find useful and thought-provoking information that resonates with you and helps smooth your road. Best wishes to you for much success and happiness over the years to come!

Some quotes from both unknown and successful people in their field may also be helpful.

All our dreams can come true if we have the courage to pursue them.

—Walt Disney

You will never feel 100 percent ready when an opportunity arises. So just do it.

—Unknown

One of the greatest gifts you can give yourself, right here, right now, in this single, solitary, monumental moment in your life, is to decide, without apology, to commit to the journey, and not to the outcome.

—Joyce DiDonato, opera singer (Juilliard School commencement speech, 2014)

I think a lot of people dream. And while they are busy dreaming, the really happy people, the really successful people, the really interesting, engaged, powerful people, are busy doing.

—Shonda Rhimes, television producer, television and film writer, and author (Dartmouth College Commencement Speech, 2014)

You cannot dream of becoming something you do not know about. You have to learn to dream big. Education exposes you to what the world has to offer.

—Supreme Court Justice Sonia Sotomayor (commencement speech at Manhattan College, New York City, May 17, 2019)

RECOMMENDED BOOKS

If I Knew Then What I Know Now by Richard Edler

How to Win Friends and Influence People by Dale Carnegie

The Introvert Advantage—How to Thrive in an Extrovert World (If You Are an Introvert) by Marti Olsen Laney, PsyD

Seven Habits of Successful People by Steven Covey

OUR BAD. Why Practical Life Skills Are Missing, and What to Do About It by Ryan Jackson

For Men Only by Shaunti and Jeff Feldhahn (short read to better understand the opposite sex)

For Women Only by Shaunti Feldhahn (short read to better understand the opposite sex)

The One-Minute Manager by Kenneth Blanchard, PhD and Spencer Johnson, MD

The Bigs by Ben Carpenter

ABOUT THE AUTHOR

Alan L Oppenheimer, CPA, MBA, has worked for both large- and medium-size companies and experienced a variety of management styles and business situations over his forty-plus years of professional tenure. Alan also consulted for several companies in areas such as mergers and acquisitions, bankruptcy, bank loans, forecasting, and year-end audit preparation.

ACKNOWLEDGMENTS

None of this would be possible without all those who contributed their experiences gained over forty years and those who filled other support roles. Thank you to the following:

Allen Questrom	James Loomstein
Bill Mott	Jeanie Pemberton
Bill Nichols	Jeff St. Pierre
Carl Sewell	Jim Grunewald
Carlos Carpizo	Ken Myres
Chuck Larson	Keo Strull
Cindy Arlidge	Mark Jarvis
Collette Morrissey	Meg O'Malley
Daniel G. Whitsell	Phil Hill
Dave Cary	Rhonda Wrentz
David Hayden	Richard Falk
Donna Kun	Steve Rosenthal
Eric Hollerman	Tom Dubowski
Frank W. Oppenheimer	Tom Gress
Gary Pemberton	Trey Knapp
Greg Greiger	

Support Roles

Bob Weir	Jessica Knauss
Deb Silverthorn	Kandace Tyler
Debra L. Hartmann	Leslie Farin
Diane Feffer	Linda Morrissey
Gregg Jackson	Sally Fallis

www.ingramcontent.com/pod-product-compliance
Lightning Source LLC
Chambersburg PA
CBHW072002070526
44583CB00015B/1291